Ame-no-Ukihashi
天浮橋
The Ancient Martial Art of the Ninzuwu

Warlock Asylum

ISBN-10:150030428X
ISBN-13: 978-1500304287

Table of Contents

Photography by Colin Ian Bowen
Contact: ianphotoshoot@gmail.com

Cover Art by Krystian Ciechowicz
Model: Radharani Ankhara

Introduction

There are many debates and theories about the origin of what is known today as martial arts. One theme, however, remains consistent as to where these practices are said to originate. In the ancient histories of many nations, exists accounts of supernatural beings who taught the race of man the arts of combat. The Book of Enoch, an ancient Jewish religious text, dated from 300 B.C., describes the "fallen angels," Azazel and Gadreel, as the first to impart martial knowledge to early man. According to the Christian Bible, martial arts are even practiced in the heavenly realms. Daniel 10:12-14 gives an account of two angels engaged in combat.

Descriptions of Chinese martial arts can be traced to the Xia Dynasty (夏朝) which existed more than 4000 years ago. According to tradition, the Yellow Emperor, Huangdi, who is described as ascending to the throne in 2698 B.C., introduced the earliest forms of martial arts to China. The Yellow Emperor is described as a famous general who, before becoming China's leader, wrote lengthy treatises on medicine, astrology and the martial arts. He allegedly developed the practice of *jiao di* or horn-butting and utilized it in war. Many scholars now regard the Yellow Emperor as Shangdi, the highest god of the Shang Dynasty.

Many of the popular and well-respected martial art forms of today were developed by the inspiration acquired from a supernatural experience. *Knowing the Facts About the Martial Arts,* written by John Ankerberg and John Weldon, provides a detailed account of occult influences in martial arts. The book provides remarkable information on the origins of Aikido and Tai Chi:

"Aikido was developed out of Ueshiba's experience of enlightenment. In the spring of 1925, when Ueshiba was walking alone in the garden, suddenly, "a golden spirit" sprang up from the ground. "I was bathed in a heavenly light; the ground quaked as a golden cloud welled up from the earth and entered my body. I felt transformed into a golden being that filled space-I am the universe" (940:47-48). Further, "at the same time, my mind and body turned into light. I was able to understand the whispering of the birds, and was clearly aware of the mind of God...At that moment I was enlightened...I have grown to feel that the whole earth is my house, and the sun, the moon and the stars are all my own things" (920:46)

Ueshiba's meditation practice had produced in him an occult enlightenment typical of Eastern gurus and other occultists. It also produced dramatic psychic powers. Such was the occult form of "enlightenment" from which aikido sprang.

The development of Tai Chi is often credited to Chang San-Feng (ca. 1260-1368), who was apparently a Taoist hoping to discover the secret of immortality by occult means. His strong interest in the I Ching and other occult pursuits were well known and, in part, eventually led him to develop Tai Chi. The Chinese emperor himself described San-Feng as "the wise and illustrious spiritual man who understands the occult."

There is growing evidence that in support of the idea that martial arts originated from the work of the medicine man, known in other cultures as a shaman. In the book, *Bruce Lee: Fighting Spirit-A Biography,* by Bruce Thomas, observes the following on page 70:

"In the same way, the *martial arts'* animal forms *originated* from the dances of a *shaman* imbued with the animal's spirit."

The Stone Tablet: The Record of Traditional Chinese Martial Arts, published an article back in 2004, entitled, The Shamanic Fist by Ted Mancuso. The article opens with these words:

"Occasionally people take up martial arts as part of their "shamanic" quest. Of course such a thing is totally appropriate since warrior arts have long been associated with such journeys."

Martial arts originated in shamanism. There is a popular legend that the Shaolin monks developed martial arts by their observation of the "animals" and were able to adapt methods of defense based on their movements. This is a half-truth if taken literally. Let us look a little bit further into this legend.

Martial arts developed alongside Traditional Chinese Medicine. It wasn't literal "animals" that the Shaolin monks were observing, but the "wheel of animals," the zodiac. It was through their communion with the stars that they received certain knowledge in dreams and astral projection. Watching the animals is really a metaphor that was symbolic of communing with the constellations of the zodiac. We can be certain that this was the case because this is how the science of acupuncture was developed.

Each constellation in the zodiac represents a section of the human body. The monks were able to commune with the stars and could tell the nature of the physical body by understanding the stars that were in the corresponding constellation of a certain part of the anatomy. The light from these different stars dictated the "metals" that were used for the needles in acupuncture. It was during the development of this science that martial arts were created.

Martial arts, like acupuncture, is a healing science. While Traditional Chinese Medicine focuses on healing by relieving blockages in the meridians in order to balance the movement of "chi energy," martial arts was created as a form of exorcism by which a person can be healed.

In ancient times, criminals and people who randomly attacked others were viewed as individuals possessed by wandering spirits, a widely-held opinion among shamans and spiritualists that still exists today. Wandering spirits were once human beings that died accidentally, painfully, and "wander" the earth seeking to attach themselves to the spiritually-weak so they can enjoy some of the delights of the physical world. The possessed person is then led into a world of crime, or may inflict pain upon others. It is due to the folly orchestrated by wandering spirits that martial arts were developed.

The same acupuncture points that are used in Chinese Medicine were now used to exorcise a wandering spirit by means of punches and strikes. If the spirit had permanently taken over the body, the martial artist may have had to execute a series of "death blows" in order to release the spirit from this physical realm. In this, we learn that the true purpose of martial arts was for healing and exorcism. Today, there are a lot of people who study self-defense while the number of martial artists has declined. We can say the same for yoga, a one-time spiritual practice that is growing, but only for its physical benefits. Self-defense is self-defense, but fighting is the last option for any true martial artist.[1]

---

[1] Information regarding the origin of martial arts was widely suppressed, not because of its shamanistic beginnings, but was mainly due to the fact that these shamans were women.

The Legend of Yuki Onna

In order to understand the ancient martial tradition of, we must begin by examining the legend of Yuki-onna.

Yuki-onna (Snow Woman) is a well-known yokai appearing in Japanese folklore. She is described as a tall, beautiful woman with long black hair and blue lips, appearing on snowy nights, some say during the full moon. Her extremely pale, in some cases transparent skin, makes it easy to blend in with the snowy landscape. She is said to wear a white kimono or can appear nude.

There are many stories surrounding Yuki-onna, but her description seems to vary as different regions in Japan seem to have a slightly different perspective of this entity than the other. There is, however, a consistent theme of a Yuki-onna preying upon travelers who are trapped in snowstorms. She can use her breath to freeze them to death or lead them astray as they die of overexposure to cold temperatures. In a Wikipedia article, under the title Yuki-onna, we read:

"Other times, she manifests holding a child. When a well-intentioned soul takes the "child" from her, they are frozen in place. Parents searching for lost children are particularly susceptible to this tactic. Other legends make Yuki-onna much more aggressive. In these stories, she often invades homes, blowing in the door

with a gust of wind to kill residents in their sleep (some legends require her to be invited inside first).

What Yuki-onna is after varies from tale to tale. Sometimes she is simply satisfied to see a victim die. Other times, she is more vampiric, draining her victims' blood or "life force." She occasionally takes on a succubus-like manner, preying on weak-willed men to drain or freeze them through sex or a kiss.

Like the snow and winter weather she represents, Yuki-onna has a softer side. She sometimes lets would-be victims go for various reasons. In one popular Yuki-onna legend, for example, she sets a young boy free because of his beauty and age. She makes him promise never to speak of her, but later in life, he tells the story to his wife who reveals herself to be the snow woman. She reviles him for breaking his promise, but spares him again, this time out of concern for their children (but if he dares mistreat their children, she will return with no mercy. Luckily for him, he is a loving father). In some versions, she chose not to kill him because he told her, which she did not treat as a broken promise (technically, Yuki-Onna herself is not a human, and thus did not count."

While some descriptions of Yuki-onna may appear to be horrific, there is evidence to support that she is an ancient goddess that was prominently worshipped during the Jomon period. Careful study of the Yuki-onna legend aligns her with the ancient Mesopotamian Inanna/Ishtar.[2]

Yuki-onna is a spirit associated with snow. Inanna/Ishtar's sacred color is white. Yuki-onna is noted for her remarkable beauty, sometimes said to spare the life of her prey, due to their age and how handsome they were. She is beautiful as fresh snowfall, but deadly as the cold can be. Inanna/Ishtar is described as the Goddess of Love and War.

January 2nd is the birthday of the ancient Sumerian goddess Inanna. During this time it was believed that the first dream of the New Year casted either a benevolent or malevolent fate for the recipient. *The Japan Encyclopedia* describes Yuki-onna as a Toshigami (歳神), a special deity that appeared on specific days and brought either good or bad fortune for the coming year.

Ninzuwu-Shinto records describe Yuki-Onna as an ancient goddess of a particular martial art style called Ame-no-Ukihashi . She is often portrayed as having no feet, floating across the snow, leaving no footprints, (a feature of many Japanese ghosts). She can also shape-shift, transforming into a cold mist or a burst of snow. These descriptions have a very deep esoteric meaning, as we read about in the Ivory Tablets of the Crow:

---

2 Ancient Chinese goddess Xi Wangmu is associated with the tiger and the color white. She was originally an avenging goddess of calamity and plague. During the Han Dynasty, however, she became associated with immortality and was a teacher of the sages.

"And the Bride of Nyarzir has the body of a beautiful woman wearing a white dress without legs."

Another aspect of Yuki-onna that we find in the Art of Ninzuwu teachings is her ability to feed off the life-force of her victims. In the Ivory Tablets of the Crow, we read:

"Upon seeing the Sword of the Ninzuwu, the Fahmu will inquire about your passage and the way you came upon this dream. You must answer with the following mantra……It means "fire-life eat."

Another reference about the ancient rite of Yuki-onna can be found in the Ivory Tablets of the Crow's account of how Nudzuchi met Xuz:

"Xuz took refuge in a cave, hoping that the *cold wind* would cease and fell asleep with only a portion of food for day left,…..Shortly after, a woman appeared with a fresh pot of stew in her hands and a drawn sword. She was a beautiful maiden with long black hair and full lips, like the flowers that last for one season……Xuz took the woman, whose name is …Lady of Heaven, the Warrior-Priestess, as his wife."

The Art of Ninzuwu is said to be founded by the Tengu. The knowledge of how this came about is featured in a few articles appearing on the Art of Ninzuwu blog page. The reader is advised to review these writings at their own convenience. Our language, Vasuh, and many of our practices are based on rites sacred to the Tengu and the energies of the Ryugu-jo. Bob Curran, in the *Encyclopedia of the Undead*, states the following concerning Yuki-onna:

"Although Hearn described her as a type of ghost, the idea of the Snow Woman was probably much older than the folklore that he had heard. In some parts of Japan, the Yuki Onna was described as a form of the tengu, very ancient Japanese demons."

According to the Art of Ninzuwu teachings, Yuki-onna was a class of warrior-priestesses who were named after the founder of their lineage and were known to train in the snow and severe cold. Their martial art style was entirely mystical in its approach.

Many of the writings in the Ninzuwu tradition describe the Tengu as protectors of the Shinto faith. In like manner, Yuki-onna protected forests and other natural forms from predators during their winter sleep, which explains why her prey is often described as men seeking to fell trees. The Tengu were said to inhabit certain trees, specifically, those of cedar and pine. Other deities in Shinto mythology were also said to exist in trees.

Earlier in our discussion, we spoke about the similarities between Yuki-onna and Dingir Ishtar. The Shinto equivalent of Dingir Ishtar is Ame-no-

Uzume-no-Mikoto. Ame-no-Uzume-no-Mikoto is widely known as the deity who played an important role in luring Amaterasu Ohkami out of the rock-cave. In another myth, she escorts Ninigi-no-Mikoto to the Central Land of Reed Plains. The Encyclopedia of Shinto states the following about Ame-no-Uzume-no-Mikoto:

"Kogo shūi notes that Uzume's behavior on this occasion was the origin for the ceremony of spirit-pacification (chinkonsai), a religious service performed by the Sarume clan. In addition to her role as patron kami of actors and other performing arts, Uzume is also viewed as having the role of negotiator with new, unknown beings. Ninigi-no-Mikoto sent her to confront and ascertain the identity of the kami Sarutahiko, who stood at the border between the Plain of High Heaven and the Central Land of Reed Plains. In an "alternate writing" recorded in Nihongi, it is stated that the other kami were fearful of Sarutahiko's weird appearance, and refused to meet with him, but Uzume bared her breasts and approached him with a derisive laugh. Thereafter, the two kami shared the role of guide for Ninigi as he proceeded on his descent, and Uzume accompanied Sarutahiko to his resting place in Ise upon completion of his role. In recognition of her service to the Heavenly Grandchild, Uzume was granted a new name based on Sarutahiko's, thus becoming Sarume no kimi, or chief of the Sarume clan.

According to Kojiki, while in Ise, Uzume made

the fish swear obeisance to the Heavenly Grandchild; only the mouth-less sea cucumber did not speak, so Uzume used a knife to cut a slit in it for mouth. In this episode, the Sarume no kimi are thus portrayed as being the first to receive offerings at Ise.

In addition, another "alternate writing" transmitted by Nihongi notes that it was Uzume who warned Amaterasu of Susanoo's reapproach to the Plain of High Heaven after he had once been banished. Kogo shūi explains the origin of Uzume's name as meaning a "fearsome and courageous woman," but her divine personality was related more to the superiority of laughter and harmony than to confrontation and trepidation based on overwhelming strength. Further, based on the fact that the Chinese character forkanzashi (hair pin) is used in her name to indicate uzu, the name may have originated from words relating to the hair pins and other accoutrements worn by a divine medium (see miko)."

When Ninigi-no-Mikoto, the grandson of Amaterasu Ohkami, was venturing into the Central Land of Reed Plains he encountered Sarutahiko Okami, an earthly deity of awesome appearance. Ame-no-Uzume-no-Mikoto was able to pacify what may have been a "would-be-conflict" between Ninigi-no-Mikoto and Sarutahiko Okami. The result was that both, Sarutahiko Okami and Ame-no-Uzume-no-Mikoto, shared in guiding Ninigi-no-Mikoto during his descent. *"Ame-no-Uzume-no-*

Mikoto was granted a new name based on Sarutahiko's, thus becoming Sarume no kimi, or chief of the Sarume clan," as mentioned in the information cited in the Encyclopedia of Shinto. W. G. Aston writes the following footnote concerning Ame-no-Uzume-no-Mikoto's title of Sarume-no-Kimi:

"The Sarume were primarily women who performed comic dances (sarumahi or monkey-dance) in honour of the Gods. They are mentioned along with the Nakatomi and Imbe as taking part in the festival of first-fruits and other Shinto ceremonies. These dances were the origin of the Kagura and No performances. Another function of the Sarume is that indicated in the part taken by Uzume no Mikoto when the Gods enticed the Sun-Goddess out of her rock-cave. She is there said to have been divinely inspired. This divine inspiration has always been common in Japan. The inspired person falls into a trance, or hypnotic state, in which he or she speaks in the character of some God. Such persons are now known as Miko, defined by Hepburn as a woman who, dancing in a Miya, pretends to hold communication with the Gods and the spirits of the dead,' in short a medium."

Aston notes how the rites of Uzume-no-Mikoto are observed, in part, by the miko, who served today as shrine maidens, but the term originally was applied to female shamans of ancient times. Miko often appear in a white kimono. One of the traditional tools of the miko is a gehōbako, or the supernatural box that contains dolls, animal and human skulls and Shinto prayer beads.

Sarutahiko Okami takes Ame-no-Uzume-no-Mikoto as his wife. Interestingly, Saruahiko Okami is considered by some to be the ancestor of the Tengu. Based on the information we have covered so far, we can discern the origins of the Yuki-onna from sources not associated with the Art of Ninzuwu's teachings. Yuki-onna was a warrior-class of priestesses, which were later known as the miko. These priestesses were adept in the magical arts, but were able to understand the astrological movements of the celestial bodies.

We can be certain that Yuki-onna represents an older class of priestesses, associated with Uzume-no-Mikoto, who later became known as miko, based on the myth of Amaterasu Ohkami emerging from the rock-cave. The emergence of Amaterasu Ohkami from the rock-cave had to take place during the winter solstice, the rebirth of the sun. This would mean that the dance of Ame-no-Uzume-no-Mikoto was a winter solstice dance. Ame-no-Uzume-no-Mikoto is relative to Yuki-onna.

In the same way that Ame-no-Uzume-no-Mikoto married Sarutahiko Okami, it is very well possible that the power of the ancient Japanese shamaness derived from the Tengu and other kami. The Encyclopedia of Shinto, under the subject Fugeki, states:

"A fugeki is believed capable of summoning a divine spirit or the spirit of a deceased person to descend into his or her body and mind, which both spontaneously and deliberately become the site to which the spirit descends; this process is called hyōi ("possession"). Such a religious figure is called a "shaman," although, since he or she serves as an intermediary to the world of divine or deceased spirits, he or she could be called a "medium" (reibai). ....The Treatise on the Wa People (Woren zhuan; J. Wajinden) section of The Official History of Wei (Weizhi; J. Gishi) describes Himiko as a woman who skillfully captivated people through sorcery (kidō 鬼道).... Line drawings on earthenware fragments dating back to the Yayoi period show a person raising both arms as if to fly and wearing a costume with what appear to be outspread wings. The person in this bird costume is presumed to be a priest officiating at a ceremony for the community. The appearance of a bird[3] was probably assumed by the priest to conduct the ceremony because birds were believed to be the bearers of spirits of grains (kokurei) and ancestral spirits (sorei). A figurine excavated from the Shimizudani ruins in Nara

---

3 Birds are symbolic of immortality and a symbol of the soul. The Ivory Tablets of the Crow is an excellent example of this. In the book A Taoist Path to Immortality, we read: "The Chinese ideogram for "immortal" (hsien) depicts a man and a mountain, suggesting a hermit; the older form of hsien, however, shows a man dancing around, flapping his sleeves like wings. To become immortal is to be "transformed Into a feathered being." Image comes from the mythology of eastern Chinese tribes who claimed bird ancestors, worshipped bird deities, and held religious rites with bird dances performed on stilts. The affinity of the Taoist immortals to birds (crane, phoenix, magpie, stork, or raven) is a persistent theme in iconography and legend."

Prefecture has a deer drawn on its chest that is hypothesized to have been offered as a sacrifice or regarded as a spirit of the land. An artifact from the Karako-Kagi ruins, also in Nara Prefecture, has female genitals drawn on the bottom half of its body. Though whether or not the figurine depicts a person who will conduct a harvest rite is uncertain, the figurine does appear to be a female priest."

When ancient Japan moved from a matriarchal society, ruled by female shamans, Himiko is an example of this, to a patriotic system, many of the practices of the ancient shamaness were deemed evil. Yuki-onna would appear at will as she represented the living shade of these ancient priestesses who now served as gatekeepers of the invisible realm.

Yuki-onna is represented by several forces in the Ninzuwu pantheon, but most-prominently as the Ayaqox. In the Ivory Tablets of the Crow, we read:

"Her dwelling place is full of clouds and flashes of lightening. It is said that even the ground she walks on will appear as the clouds of heaven."

Another reference to Yuki-onna found in the Ivory Tablets of the Crow is Wutzki, which is described as a "cosmic fire." Wutzki and Yuki-onna are equivalent in terms of Simple and English Gematria:

Yuki Onna in English   (y   u   k   i   _   o   n   n   a)

Gematria Equals: 660

$$\underline{}0\underline{}$$
150 126 66 54   90 84 84 6

Yuki Onna in Simple
Gematria Equals: 110

$$(\quad \overset{\text{y u k i}}{\underline{}}0\overset{\text{o n n a}}{\underline{}}\quad)$$
25 21 11 9   15 14 14 1

Wutzki in English
Gematria
Equals: 660

$$(\quad \overset{\text{w u t z k i}}{\underline{}}\quad)$$
138 126 120 156 66 54

Wutzki in Simple Gematria
Equals: 110

$$(\quad \overset{\text{w u t z k i}}{\underline{}}\quad)$$
23 21 20 26 11 9

It is interesting to note that both Wuzki and Yuki-onna equal 660 and 110. If we reduce these two numbers to a single digit we get 3 (660 = 6 + 6 + 0 = 12, 1 +2 = 3) and 2 (110 = 1 + 1 = 2). In the Vasuh language, three represents Tuu, which is symbolic of Tsukiyomi-no-Mikoto, a lunar deity. 2 is symbolic of Amaterasu Ohkami, who some describe as a solar deity. Therefore, in Yuki-onna and Wutzki are the powers of the Sun and Moon. 2 + 3 = 5. Five equals Bnhu in the Vasuh language. Five also represents Owatatsumi-no-Mikoto and initiation into the rites of the Dragon Palace. The Ivory Tablets of the Crow states:

"Every battle is a creation. There is only one palace. It is the Dragon, but it is called the Gate of Death in error by many who do not understand."

The term Wutzki itself refers to the 'master-shaman of life-force energy." Wu is a Chinese term for shaman, which in Japanese is miko. Wu is also the

word for crow in Chinese. Tzu, or Tz, is a title
meaning "master" in Chinese. Ki is Japanese for
chi, or vital energy. Many of the words in the
Vasuh language are a combination of Chinese,
Indian, Japanese, and Sumerian terms, as these
languages originated from the Proto-Afro-Asiatic
language of the Empire of Mu.

History of the use of the martial way of Yuki-onna,
Ame-no-Ukihashi, can be seen in the example of
the onna-bugeisha. The onna-bugeisha are often
described as female warriors who were members of
the samurai class in feudal Japan. Famous among
these were Empress Jingu and Tomoe Gozen.

While their association with the samurai is often
noted in history, little information is available
about their mysterious arts, which could paralyze
an opponent without the touch of hands. These
methods were inherited from a peculiar class of
mike that say certain incantations while performing
martial katas.

The martial stances of the ancient shamaness were
taught in secret and by the use of a set of letters and
symbols. The movement of chi energy can be
taught and weighed by the shapes of letters, which
were symbolic of certain body postures. These
letters were known as onna-de, or woman's hand,
among the onna-bugeisha, which later became
known as hiragana script.

Jokwa is an ancient Japanese goddess that may
have been an influential force in the workings of

the ancient shamans of Japan. A further investigation into the origin of this term reveals the legacy of this ancient goddess, who held various names in many lands.. Nathaniel Altman, in a book entitled, Sacred Water: The Spiritual Source of Life, states:

"In Chinese myth, the *goddess Nu Kua* (also known as *Jokwa* in Japan) fought against the giants and demons who were held responsible for the flood, and stopped the rising waters by loading the riverbanks with charred reeds. After the flood subsided, Nu Kua created an army of powerful dragons to maintain order in the world."

Altman clearly identifies Jokwa as the Japanese name of the goddess Nu Kua. Nu Kua, also called Nuwa is one of the oldest deities in Chinese history, best known for creating mankind and repairing the wall of heaven. She is portrayed as half-woman and half-snake. On some occasions, she appears as half-woman and half-dragon.

Nuwa and her husband, described as her brother in some accounts, Fu Xi, are said to have survived a "great flood." Afterwards they procreated, which led to the procreation of human beings. Ironically, Fu Xi is credited to have discovered the Yi Jing. The Yi Jing Apocrypha of Genghis Khan, states the following:

"Barbara G. Walker reveals some very valuable information concerning the Yi Ching, in her book,

The I Ching of the Goddess. On page 14 of the said work, she writes:

"Older Asian systems attributed to the Goddess, not the God, every type of logical system for expressing cycles of time and space, including calendars, time measurements by astrological observation...It was said that Fu His was the god as a brother-consort of this primal Goddess who brought all things into being and delegated some of her authority to him....The story that the Goddess gave the I Ching to the cultural hero points to the likelihood that this symbol system- like other systems of ideograms, numbers, calendars, alphabets, measurements, and hieroglyphics- was originated by women in a matriarchal age, when men served chiefly as hunters, warriors, and field hands while women evolved more civilized skills."

Nuwa was known in ancient Chinese mythology as a creator deity. Some even consider her to be the first ruler of China. Is it really possible that Fu Xi could have gotten such knowledge from Nuwa? It seems very probable and may lead us into another discovery.... We can learn something a bit deeper by if we look into the origin of the name of Fu Xi's wife, *Nuwa*. It is well known that female shamans held positions of authority during the matriarchal age. The name Nuwa is composed of two parts, *Nu*, meaning female and *Wa*, the ancient name for Japan. This would mean that the brother-sister, sibling marriage between Fu Xi and Nuwa is symbolic of an era when China and Japan were ruled by a joint force. Nuwa, or Lady of Japan bestowed the knowledge of the Yi Jing to China…. Interestingly, the goddess Xi Wangmu is also associated with Nuwa. She "governs the internal structure of the nine heavens and regulates yin and yang," and has domain over the Big Dipper. This would make her closely connected with the Vasuh language, appearing in the Ivory Tablets of the Crow."

Dr. Christina Miu Bing Cheng, in a paper presented to the 17th Triennial Congress of the International Comparative Literature Association, August 8-15, 2004, in Hong Kong, entitled, *Matriarchy at the Edge: The Mythic Cult of Nu Wa* 女媧 *in Macau*, wrote:

"The "degrading" transformation of Nu Wa from the supreme goddess to the consort of Fu Xi may speak for the gradual social change from matriarchal society to patriarchal society in ancient China. In the Nu Wa Temple in Macau, however, her somewhat subordinate status as Fu Xi's wife cannot be traced. She is still honoured as Repairer of Heaven and Mother Goddess, thus retaining her matriarchal greatness. In the heyday of Macau, Nu Wa was popularly venerated and the temple well patronized. What then was the divine intervention? Formerly there were many prostitutes, especially in Rua da Felicidade 福隆新街 — a red light district. It is gathered that prostitutes used to go to pray to this matriarchal deity for protection from venereal diseases and gynaecological problems (Tang, 1994:208). They would naturally pray to return to a "normal" life, and to find "proper" husbands. Hence, Nu Wa has come to be a quasi patroness of prostitutes in Macau. In this respect, her role is similar to that of Ishtar, the great Babylonian goddess of love, sex, and fertility.[4] As the goddess of fertility and bestower of children, she is mostly honoured by barren women who would pray for children, and in particular, for male heirs for the continuity of the family tree. Given the myth that she repaired the heavens, broken-hearted worshippers would pray to her to repair their *qing tian* 情天 (love heaven). By and large, she is mainly worshipped as the Goddess of Marriage and the Goddess of Match-making 媒神 in Macau. It is plain to see Nu Wa's divine roles have been re-shaped and modified in response to the interests and preoccupations of the people there."

Nuwa compares greatly to Johuta, as they are both associated with nine realms and are described as a crow in some mythologies. Nuwa, however, was known as a creatrix-goddess of fertility and marriage. It seems that she may have been demonized in the stories of the Yuki-onna. One can see this clearly in the legend of Oyazu.

Despite the horrific description of Yuki-onna, the account of Oyazu reveals a different side of the Snow Maiden. It shows us how a Yuki-onna was able to serve a beneficial purpose. Oyazu was a

---

4 Ishtar (this is her Akkadian name) was called Inanna by the Sumerians, and venerated as Mother Goddess. However, she was also a War Goddess, often referred to as "the Lady of Battles".

woman whose spirit appeared to Kyuzaemon, wife of Isaburo. She appeared at the home of Kyuzaemon and prayed before his family shrine. She told Kyuzaemon that her husband, Isaburo, had left her parents without support when she died and she wanted to correct this wrong. Next day, Kyuzaemon found that Isaburo had returned to his in-laws, having been visited by his wife's spirit in the guise of Yuki-Onna.

This depiction of Yuki-Onna in the account of Oyazu, is similar to what is described in the Zhong Lü Chuan Dao Ji as a Celestial Immortal. The account describes Oyazu with the ability to manifest in the vicinity of an altar, but also travel great distances in the work of virtue. Spirit immortals who are summoned to heaven are given the minor office of water realm judge. Over time, they are promoted to oversee the earthly realm and finally become administrators of the celestial realm. These immortals have the power to travel back and forth between the earthly and celestial realms.

In the Art of Ninzuwu teachings, what is often described as a Yuki-onna, is seen as an ancient goddess, Ame-no-Ukihashi-hime-no-Mikoto, that was demonized by an opposing priesthoods. This force has several names, depending on its function.

Book of the Mirrors

The Snow Maiden will appear when Heaven and Earth are at rest, for this is the true meaning of her name. Look! Wood has lost its foliage! Look! Water is frozen and is of no service to anyone! Look! The Earth is covered by the frozen rain! Look! The Fire cannot grow due to the shortness of its breath! Look! The Air has indeed grown heavy! See how the Snow Maiden easily expresses her dominion over the elements that men has put faith in! The true nature of these things can only be understood in Dreams, when the mind can travel beyond the perception of experience and the body is in the season of winter.

This message will come to thee as the soft rain upon the scale of dimensions. Surely, winter is the only season known in other parts of the universe. It is the summer of otherworldly things. Are not the stars in Heaven like snowflakes of light descending upon the Earth that we call gravity? Winter is the womb, for all things are born out of meditation. What is Fire on Earth is Water in Heaven and what is Water in Heaven is Fire on Earth. Winter is the boundary of the mind.

They, however, enjoy the lust of Heaven and Earth. When the trees are blooming, when the fruit is made ripe, when the harvest begins, these are all seasons unto themselves, but are not separate from each other. These seasons are expressions of lust, the passion procured from the intercourse held between Heaven and Earth. We say that what is alive is not truly alive, but is only animated by the celestial dance of lust. When the fragrance of lust comes to pass, the life that derives from it will perish.

Enjoy all the seasons. They are good medicine for the body and are useful places to earn thy position in life. Know too, that winter is a Dream and that the life of the common man is only a dream within the Mind of Winter. Winter is the Dream, a dimension that the starry realms are contained in. It holds the four seasons within its womb. One season, by which its name is called acts as a gate for the uninitiated to enter. This is the meaning of winter. Winter is only a gate to the Void.

How can life be more than just a simple desire? How am I to understand these things? Is not the absence of existence found in the cold? A perfect description of the three seasons is in the three questions. Now we shall hear the Sermon of Yuki-onna.

The cold air is filled with gold, bricks of life-force ripe in due season. The frozen essence of vitality I give unto you. Remember, what is Fire on Earth is Water in Heaven and what is Water in Heaven is Fire on Earth. Drink from the Fountain of Life! Did you not ask the Shamuzi to lead you to such a dream? This is that Dream my child. Gather the treasure around you! Only a few can see it or understand where to find it. Remember that in each Dream is a map, a way to step out of the cycle of lust and laugh at its innocence.

Be as the Gatekeepers in each and every experience. You do not have to look for them, they are all around you. Feel the Wind and adjust your perception. On your journeys, acknowledge the plants and trees in your experience before giving notice to the people who walk by you. Look at the trees in your experience. Greet them with your mind. Take note of their expressions. Examine their leaves, knowing it is their face of many faces. They are your kin, much more than the men and women who you seek to impress. The trees breed the air we breathe. In labor, they produce food for us to eat. Why let your mind be clouded by men and women who cannot do such things? Think of the trees as one of your own. Practice these things on your journeys for it is a form of meditation that reveals the place of the Dream.

The mind of trees can travel long distances while people are rooted in their experiences. Trees draw in Water from Earth and Fire from Heaven. Man draws in Fire from Earth, desires from his experiences, and Water from Heaven, or emotions from his thoughts. How can Water be drawn from the Earth and Fire from Heaven? How can Fire be drawn from the Earth and Water from Heaven? It is the kiss of two mirrors facing each other and like many things, said to be alive, is logically ignorant of the process. Within intuition access to other worlds can be gained merely by the reflection within itself. There is no truth for a logical origin of the universe.

Mirrors are created to reflect an appearance. What more are appearances than the intentions of Heaven and Earth? Mirrors are frozen Water. They are the season of reflection. Man draws in Fire from Earth and Water from Heaven. Trees draw in Water from Earth and Fire from Heaven. Yet, man and the tree are both ignorant of the process. Although it is a vital process for the existence of men and trees alike, these things are inspired by unseen forces unknown to either man or the tree, but can be seen in the mirror.

A mirror is an action. It is one treasure of Yuki-Onna. When a person acknowledges plants and trees in their experience before giving notice to the people who pass them by, they are looking into the mirror. The mirror is frozen Water. Frozen water over the Earth appears as ice and snow. What then is the ice and the snow? They are emotions without desires, a form of life-force energy that is gained from the cold.

After these things had occurred, a rebellious gesture stood up amidst the sea of thoughts and emotions in the form of a question. *"What are we to profit from the words of a Yuki-Onna? I want to stay warm and comfortable!"* The noise of laughter was heard loudly throughout the congregation of thoughts.

My initiation is rare. They study techniques and strange dances, which often imitate animals. And these things are fine among themselves. There will come a time, however, where those who practice such things must fight against them. They will become a limitation, as all forms of imitation are.

First, look at yourself in the mirror. See the mechanicalness of desire. The mirror is important because many will deceive themselves into believing that they are on the path. They will make every excuse to align themselves with what they were impressed by! Is this not the beginning of lust?

The ego is used as a mirror by many, and those who look into it are blinded by its fabric. Not only is it blinding, but it demands that one relinquish their own Self. What can one drop of Water do for an ocean? How much value is one grain of sand on a beach? What attention can one star receive over the vast multitude of dangling lights in Heaven? There is nothing that these things can do on their own accord, but the ego will insist otherwise. The ego can easily be known as it is always glorifying the difference. And the difference is always the result. This is how one becomes aware of the ego, so they can resist its power, which is nothing. Nothing can mean a lot to a person with the wrong ideas. Few can let go of such things.

Many people will hold on to certain ideas in their youth. They perceive a world that is tragic and search for some secret power, quests of the ego at large. These things are fruitless! Cultivate love! How can the meaning of existence be understood? As the Creator was inspired by love to share the experience of existence with other expressions of life. You so feebly stand up in the face of the Void wondering how you can be of help without knowing the meaning of existence. If you really are a question, then you know very well that an answer can kill you. It is not a question of right and wrong. These things came upon their own accord. A raindrop can't do anything on its own. When it is merged with the divine quality of love, however, all things are possible.

Book of the White Candle

Take heed in the knowledge of the white candle
that burns, for it is another tool of the Yuki-onna.
Some say that a lit white candle is sunshine on ice.
The wax melting away, are the years of our life.
How can a candle burn without the wax melting?
This is the equation of immortality! What is
immortality really?

We are all suns. Suns embody principles as they
shine out into the experience of matter. We are the
embodiment of universal principles. No principle
remains consistent forever. Principles change
because Heaven and Earth are in constant motion.
The changes in Heaven and Earth causes change in
the principles that we see all around us, namely
creation. Existence is motion. It is constant change.
Existence is the consciousness of life and death.
Any principle that seeks to gain immortality
through existence is a fool. Immortality cannot be
gained on the level of existence, for existence is the
cycle of life and death. Nothing that exists can
escape this cycle. What was once a young boy, is
now a man of old age. If a boy remains a boy, it is
perceived as something unnatural, an illness of
sorts. When a boy grows into a man, it is not by his
own desire that he came to be a man. The boy did
not invoke the height he has as a man. The boy did
not invoke his own puberty, but puberty comes
upon the boy by an invisible force that has reigns

over existence. Everything is happening. Everything is changing and these changes are not created by the will of man. So how can man become immortal if he can't control the changes that his own body is subject to?

There was once a gardener who brought delight to all who attended the king's garden. People came from distant lands to see the beautiful array of flowers, plants and trees. Every day the gardener would cultivate the garden's soil, nurturing and pruning the plants and trees. It was said too that the garden brought good fortune to the king and his dominion. His kingdom, and its subjects, was regarded with great honor by the surrounding nations. Every citizen bathed in the shadow of their own fig tree. It was known that throughout the whole kingdom, and among the surrounding nations, that such fortune came from the talisman of the garden, that being in how it was arranged. This fortune lasted for quite some time.

Years passed, the gardener became subject to the designs of evil spirits. It was for this reason that he grew tired of caring for the garden. His reasoning soon began to follow the logic of evil spirits. The gardener convinced himself that caring for the garden was a source of harm, as millions of insects would lose their lives. The gardener lamented how his nurturing and pruning caused pain and suffering for the plants and trees. Up until this time, the gardener had enjoyed every luxury that life had to offer. The king had assigned two merchants to attend to his needs. Any expense that was incurred by the gardener was paid for by the king. The gardener now demanded money from the king and refused to give the garden special care, only doing a few things.

Bad luck fell over the king and his kingdom due to the gardener's actions. People began to suffer from disease and pestilence. After long protests of lamenting and worrying about the insects, the gardener's health began to fail. He died of stroke shortly after. The garden had long since been overrun and the flowers, plants, and trees, were all consumed by the insects that deceived the gardener. The king and his kingdom were crushed by the surrounding nations, and every citizen was put to death. The garden was no more. The king and his kingdom was no more. The insects remained for a short time until winter came, dying upon its arrival.

If you can find humanity in the Story of the Gardener, then you can find immortality. It could be that humanity is like the insects in the garden. They do not know why they are a part of the garden, but are concerned only for their own survival, even if it means the life of the whole garden. These insects will even perform evil deeds like begging to some god, which in this case would be the gardener, that their lives are saved above all other creations in existence.

There are others who will reason that humanity can be found in the example of the gardener. The gardener is the man of the five senses. He cannot see that the cycle of life and death must occur in order to nurture the beauty of the higher worlds. Man, like the gardener, will become obsessed with issues that may seem correct for the ordinary man, but is not in line with the will of Heaven and Earth. His helpful contributions are some of Heaven's most accursed sins. He is a pawn of evil spirits for he seeks to judge himself and others without knowing the will of Heaven and Earth.

Many will liken the condition of humanity to the people that lived in the gardener's kingdom. They live their lives without care or want, only enjoying the beauty of the garden. It can even be said that the people of the kingdom could have cared for the garden after the gardener fell ill and saved the prosperity of their own kingdom. They were, however, too busy with life's concerns.

Finally, there are those who will equate humanity with the king. The king observes everything around him for the benefit of himself and his subjects. While he may acknowledge the influence of unseen phenomena over the material world, he is no different than the people of his kingdom. He holds his responsibility with honor. He is free from blame.

The principles are not immortal, but surrenders to the purpose from which it owes its existence. Regardless of the reason, principles are subject to change. What kingdom lasts forever? Is there a man who walks among us today that was present during the founding of the country that we live in?

We know the answer to these questions, but the influence of evil spirits will deceive us into thinking otherwise. Immortality is not found in the dimension of existence. The true immortal is the talisman of the garden, as it absorbed and was nurtured by the energy of every character in the parable.

During sleep the mind sees its thoughts as dreams. These dreams are produced by the shared mind, but during sleep they feel so real. Many of us will identify with their existence, as it seems so real. The quality of our dreams affect the health of the mind and vice-versa. Our existence is a dream in the mind of the universe, a thought dancing between two poles. When we procure the extraterrestrial dimension of love into our live, we awaken in a much healthier condition when we awaken. When we awaken, we are one. We are a whole universe. Life was extended to us with the same trust that a droplet of water is given by an ocean, endeavoring to remain pure in order to have the ability to attach itself to the whole with the same clarity. If these things are difficult to understand, then just remember a lit white candle.

When the wax of a white candle has melted, the fire will die out. This is the garden. If the flame of the white candle is extinguished before its wax has melted, it will be disregarded. This is the gardener. The gardener, the king, the people, and the insects are all part of the wax. The fire is the will of Heaven and Earth. The hand that lit the fire is the divine spark within, the unnamable one of the void. This is the Book of the White Candle.

The Book of the Five Petals of a Rose

These are the customs and the knowledge procured from the cultivation of the vital energy. In the examples, as with the ones prior, the practitioner should examine how the energy moves and learn its nature. It is written in the Ivory Tablets of the Crow:

"And surely the Magicians of the Secret Lands, not known to men, study well these words, and those who observe them."

We are babes to this knowledge in comparison to the magicians that preceded us on this journey. Each petal of the rose is just and in accord with its essence. One is not to judge these paths, but know that in order to reach the higher stages of the Immortal State of Being; they must complete the step before it.

And the nature of each Immortal Kiss of the Rose is described and how the vital force moves within each circle. One cannot know immortality, if they have not studied the movement of vital energy in their own lives and experiences.

Now the Way of the Ghost Immortal is like a woman who understands the rules of courtship, but has come to know many lovers. She seeks to find something of an endless age, a very unique form of embrace. Yet, these things must be cultivated by working on a relationship, suffering through hardships together, and using adverse experiences as moments for strengthening the union.

After some time, she meets a man who is sincere and seeks to perform the necessary rites in cultivating the relationship. The woman, however, will become afraid and seek to cling to the ways of her previous lovers. She seeks her ideal love, but lives in fear of finding it. It is for this reason that she can never come to an understanding of what love is. It is the same for the Way of the Ghost Immortal.

The Ghost Immortal lives in fear of death. And there is no love of life as long as the fear of death remains in the heart. Those who follow this path will use a variety of techniques to preserve the vital force. If these techniques, however, are inspired by the fear of death, fear itself will become crystalized. When the human body fades, all that is left is fear and this is how the Ghost Immortal is born.

There is also the Way of the Secret Ghost, where certain practices can be used to cultivate the Self. These practices are not inspired by fear, but are found in the appropriate use of the "yin energy." The yin energy is that of the living shade when cultivated and seen for the sexual force that it is, the beginning of life itself. The benefits of these things are experienced in the eternal moment, a region beyond the senseless paradigm of life and death. Know that by constant application of the formulas listed herein, one will step outside the body before it folds in the arms of death and witness the tragedy painlessly, for this is the way of all immortals. And the Ghost Immortal is a necessary birth for every immortal, as it is the entry point into the realm of the eternal moment.

The Way of the Human Immortal is like a young man who seeks to make a way for himself in the world by the study of Heaven and Earth. It is through these practices that the Human Immortal learns how to overcome sickness and death. Yet, he must nourish and clothe the body.

Now the Law of Heaven and Earth becomes the mother for a son who is like a child. This type of understanding cannot see itself independent of its mother. The methods of the Human Immortal are numerous, but the mind of the Human Immortal cannot construct a thought outside of human society. They can also take the path of the Ghost or remain as they are.

The Earthly Immortal knows the Law of Heaven and Earth, also the methods of the Ghost Immortal. She uses the methods of the Human and the Ghost in a peculiar form of alchemy. The Earthly Immortal is like a woman being given into marriage. Though it is a mysterious work, she is able to emerge from the need for food and can resist cold and hot temperatures. She is immortal and of the earthly realm. If she wishes to ascend into the heavenly regions, the body must pass form.

Once the Earthly Immortal has glanced at the fruitage of a loving work, they will take a share in the realm of an unveiled reality. And the Spiritual Immortal has experienced the transmutation of the greater heart and lives in the realm of spirit. They can take on the shape and form of any object, but their work is not in the showy display of one's power. The Spiritual Immortal is like a wealthy man who feeds the poor. His work is teaching the Way of Love to those who remain on earth; and in these things, one accumulates merit for entrance into the celestial realms.

The Celestial Immortal has jurisdiction over certain portions of the physical ream. They have reached an awareness in being that is hard to grasp by the senses, save that the will of love is in its cultivation for all that is.

The Celestial Immortal is like a parent who spends their entire life performing tasks of hard labor in order to provide for their children. Immortality is work, not a belief. Very few words can be said about these paths that are actually true of its essence. All that can be said is that a rose has five petals.

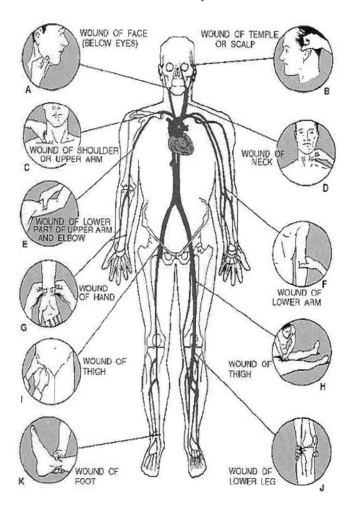

Sword of the Gathering Clouds of Heaven

Know that Yuki-onna is not the true name of the gatekeeper, but an attribute given to her priests and priestesses by their oppressors. During the Eternal Moment, being the Age of the Divine Mind, the August-Shining-One is called Ame-no-Ukihashi-hime-no-Mikoto, "Princess of the Floating Bridge of Heaven," also known as Yuki-Onna. Her priests and priestesses possessed a certain skill, known in the histories of mankind as Ame-no-Murakumo-no-Tsurugi 天叢雲剣, "Sword of the Gathering Clouds of Heaven," a technique of Ame-no-Ukihashi.

This is the Book of an Endless Age, and the magicians of the celestial realms have seen these things take place ahead of time. Be wary of those who seek "to be right" and point to certain teachings as the Way. This form of entitlement only breeds satisfaction in ordinary things. And the Way can only be found in being.

Ame-no-Murakumo-no-Tsurugi, the Cloud-Gathering Sword of Heaven, is used by the priest and priestess in their communications with the Celestial Immortals and the Spirits of the Deceased. These formulas are engraved on the walls of the Great Dragon Palace, 竜宮城, 龍宮城 Ryūgū-jō.

It has been known since ancient times that one day spent in the Dragon Palace is equal to a century. Now the Gate of Ame-no-ukihashi can be opened by those who are baptized in the ways of the Ancient One. During this time, the ways of Vasuh were learned and many days were spent in contemplation over the wondrous dreams caused by such practices. What of the language of Ut?

Know, firstly, that the languages of Vasuh and Ut are designed by the unification of Heaven and Earth. The human body is a great example of this, as every movement produced by the body, whether voluntary or involuntary, is the result of an unseen intelligence. Vasuh is the language of the subconscious mind. The language of Ut is the language of the body with all its emotional, mental, and physical characteristics.

Know, secondly, that the language of Ut, as with other languages of man, were formed and structured for the measurement of the vital energy. The vital force of every nation can be found in its language. And in the language of its nation resides the deities of that nation.

Know, thirdly, that in the celestial realms, a nation is defined, not by its national borders, or the physical characteristics of a group of people, but by the language spoken. When a king sets forth against another nation, conquering its inhabitants, he will demand that his victims learn a new language. And when a person speaks a language not inherited by Heaven, the ancestral palace, that person becomes a slave to the rulers of the said language. The words used in these languages act as gods of the slave. Now in order for the slave to acquire a favored persona in the society that he lives in, he must worship the gods of the king. And these gods are found in the languages of men and their worshippers perform great sacrifices unto them by merely speaking the language that has enslaved them.

Know, fourthly, that with each letter of a particular language, are the emotions of the ruling class. It is written in the Ivory Tablets of the Crow:

> **These kings live forever**
> **Due to the ignorant worship**
> **Of their natures**
> **Thrown about thrones**
> **These are the emotions of kings**
> **That no longer remain in the body**
> **But they dwell as emotions in all men**

> **Know that the names of these gods**
> **Are a formula**
> **A binding between the king and his earthly**
> **subject**
> **Worship not the feelings of kings**
> **Seek only initiation**
> **For initiation is the only law that is just unto man**

It is upon the Baptism of the Ancient One that the slave finds freedom, as he has learned a new language. Now the emotions of the king and queen are clothed in words and letters of various languages, existing among men. They gain prominence in the physical world by the invocation of the worshipper. When the worshipper uses the language that they are enslaved by to make an emphatic statement, the emotion is able to rise up into the realm of the subconscious mind. Once an emissary has entered this state of mind, the subconscious will then transform reality into the shape of the words it has received.

Know, fifthly, that many will be misled into thinking that they understand the nature of these things, but are indeed far removed from the mysterious essence prevalent throughout all experience. Their misunderstandings can be seen in the words they speak, which contradict the life they live. Many will claim that right and wrong are not real. They will come to adorn themselves in the beauty of such words like a person who wears a fine garment, but leads a treacherous life. When you see these things, know that they are under the spell of the king's language. And it must come to pass that these very same people engage in an internal war, while promoting that right and wrong do not exist. Now the truth in this statement can only be found among those who do not speak about such things. The realm of right and wrong, good and evil, is the place of imbalance for the vital energy. Improper circulation of life-force energy is what makes the world right and wrong, good and evil.

Know, sixthly, that the embodiment of the vital energy, life-force, is found in matter, and in the life of plants and animals, and in all that can be seen by the naked eye. All of these physical forms are patterned and shaped by the principles they represent. These principles manifest physically as matter, but are aspects of the vital energy. It is shaped into its form as it descends from Heaven. These principles are ever-changing, which is why it is said that immortality cannot be found in existence.

Know, seventhly, that immortality is found in the shape and color of the mind, as the understanding of such things is simple. Life is the migration of the vital force. The Law of Heaven and Earth is embodied in the movement of the vital force. Let the wise one then understand how to move while being still.

The Star of Ame-no-ukihashi-hime

Know that the Star of Ame-no-ukihashi-hime must be brought through the nine palaces, in a manner

similar to the Soul of Fire Prayer, during the length
of the new moon.

And the Amatsu Norito must be recited three
times. Let the Aum mudra be invoked. After these
things have taken place, recite "Ame-no-ukihashi-
hime mamori tamae sakihae tamae." Know that
these things must take place in front of the Sign of
Ame-no-ukihashi-hime, the burning of fresh pine
incense, white candles, and the Stone Bowl of
Eternity.

Remember, these are the workings of the Priest and
Priestess of Ninzuwu, a sacred dance of the soul. It
is not necessary to think of a technique, just
remember the sequence and practice the
movements, but also watch the breath and its
mantra.

These exercises are a sacred formula of legend. It is
said that these movements can stop an opponent
merely by a stare. Its working are unknown at
first, but it is a special training in how the vital
force moves. When one puts these things into
practice, the more it is understood.

The following is the language of Ut. Study these
things well. Take special care not to change what is
written herein, not even by a shadow of a letter. If
the body cannot be still, then the mind will not be
able to focus. There are many who will adorn
themselves with the fascination of words. Very few
will take the path of Johuta, for they are truly afraid
of freedom.

The Soul of Fire
(Nzu-Zhee-Nzu, Shki-Zhee-Phe)

Symbol:

The Soul of Fire is the foundation of the Art of Ninzuwu. In this world, Fire appears in Heaven and Water on Earth. Follow the course so that Water can be seen in Heaven and Fire on Earth. This stance was written about in the Age of the Gods:

"Of old, Heaven and Earth were not yet separated, and the In and Yo not yet divided. They formed a chaotic mass like an egg which was of obscurely defined limits and contained germs."[5]

---

5 Nihongi: Chronicles of Japan from the Earliest Times to A.D. 697, translated from the original Chinese and Japanese by W. G. Aston·

47

$$\text{あ} = A$$

Mantra: ah

Simplicity is the foundation of every martial science. Its mastery can be gained by following the hand in all that we do. It is written:

"The purer and clearer part was thinly drawn out, and formed Heaven, while the heavier and grosser element settled down and became Earth.

The finer element easily became a united body, but the consolidation of the heavy and gross element was accomplished with difficulty.

Heaven was therefore formed first, and Earth was established subsequently. Therefore Divine Beings were produced between them."

= I

Mantra: ee

Deity: Ama-no-toko-tachi-no-Mikoto

There is little value in technique, save the perfection of a limitation. Approach your work in discipline, for these are methods of nurturing the will. It is written:

"When Heaven and Earth began, a thing was produced in the midst of the Void, which resembled a reed-shoot. This became changed into a God,[6] who was called Ama-no-toko-tachi-no-Mikoto."

---

6 Ama-no-toko-tachi-no-Mikoto is considered by some to be the name of a primeval goddess.

う = U

Mantra: uu

Deity: Umashi-ashi-kabi-hiko-ji-no-Mikoto

A mother will use techniques to discipline and care for her children. These methods are nourishment for the will. And it is known that mothers can accomplish great deeds for the sake of their children. So it is that the will speaks in the language of martial techniques, but is not the technique itself. It is written:

"This became changed into a God, who was called Ama-no-toko-tachi-no-Mikoto. There was next Umashi-ashi-kabi-hiko-ji-no-Mikoto."

え = E

Mantra: eh

Deity: Kuni-toko-tachi-no-Mikoto

Many will debate over the light and the shadow. They fail to realize that all things must proceed forth from the Void. And to understand the Void, one must begin by taking note of the shape and color of the mind. It is written:

"There was a thing produced in the midst of the Void like floating oil, from which a God was developed, called Kuni-toko-tachi-no-Mikoto."

お = O

Mantra: oh

Deity: Ame-kagami-no-Mikoto

There are three in many ancient legends around the world. If one is allowed to read the sacred tomes of what happened before, what is, and what will come, they will see that Three is a funneled-reflection between worlds. On one side of the Three is the intercourse of Heaven and Earth. On the other side of the Three are male and female divine powers. One is a reflection of the other, and in that is a form of protection. It is written:

"Kuni-toko-tachi-no-Mikoto produced Ame-kagami-no-Mikoto."

A Slave of Immortality

Stay diligent in your work! There are many distractions that must be shed on this path, as one walks closer to knowing an Endless Age. Do not be swayed by the mechanisms of wandering spirits. Know that immortality cannot be found in existence. Existence is the world of living and dying, the changes of Heaven and Earth.

There was once a rich man who lived in the city of Auho. The man employed many slaves, but cared nothing for them. He enjoyed watching the pain that his slaves endured with pleasure. While the slaves suffered much hardship under their master, they cherished and loved the rich man.

The brutalities suffered by these slaves became a form of entertainment for all who lived in the city. Many of the villagers would bring their children down to the fields of the slaves and watch them scream in adoration for their master while being castrated. Applause filled the air when the raping of a slave woman would occur. During a certain time of year, the children of the slaves were captured and put to death by hanging. Now the number of children that were hung on the rich man's property exceeded the blades of grass that one walks upon. It was during these days that the townsmen would bring their wives to witness such events for the sake of romance. This is what was said of the rich man during his time.

Eventually, a king from a distant land got to hear of all the experiments that were being conducted by the rich slaveholder. Being appalled by such behavior, the king decided to see if the slaves really loved their master despite the suffering they experienced. The king was in shock after witnessing the affection held by the slaves for their master, the rich man. He decided to inquire the method of subjugation used by the master of the slaves. The rich man explained his methods as such:

"I just tell the slaves that I will grant them immortality if they follow me. Sometimes it's not that easy. In such instances, I will use the words of old prophets and sages for dressing up my own ideas. The slaves will see these things and begin to believe that they are working for a cause that has existed since the beginning of creation.

I do not feel guilty over how the slaves are treated because they seek immortality in this world. This tells me that these slaves are selfish. They want to use their lives, not for the improvement of life itself, but the pursuit of pleasure. No matter how difficult I make their existence, they love me even more. Maybe it is pain that they love? I am grateful nonetheless.

The passion that these slaves have for me, keeps me alive! It keeps the world they are living in alive, a place where death is inevitable. Maybe they are afraid of living in a different world? That's what makes a slave a slave.

Slavery is the business of creating and selling gods. If gods are forgotten, they will die also. Gods are a product of a slave's imagination. I am sure you know this my lord!"

The king was astonished over the slaveholder's reasoning. He took a moment to ponder over all that had been spoken. During this time, the Sun had begun its descent. The king replied:

"I feel sorry for you and your slaves. It is indeed a sad thing that they must suffer because of your ignorance. This is the end result of ignorance, worshipping ignorance. Immortality is not something that can be achieved by implementing certain exercises, or believing in some god. Gods have to die for the people that they enslave because they themselves are slaves. Any man who makes another man his slave is a slave of his own vain imaginations.

Immortality is not something that can be taught to a mortal. How can a person that can see teach a blind person? A person must recognize their own condition first. They must understand that their place in this world is not a theory.

If a man finds himself in the same world after every dream and imagination, then he can't be nothing more than his dream. His body is changing and all experience around him. Change is constant, but change is the effect and not the cause. If the cause is not known, then the purpose of life cannot be understood. If the purpose of life is not understood, then immortality becomes a form of infatuation for fatality, a pursuit more damaging to the soul than what is believed.

Immortality is a state of being. It is the course of the changeless one. There is no fear or doubt in this consciousness. Simply thinking how to avoid fear and doubt has nothing to do with what we are talking about here. Once again, many will be drawn to the study of logic, and this idea that a certain sum of things should equal the desired goal spiritually.

Just ask yourself, how can a man teach a blind man how to look into the world of experience? The man that is blind must learn how to see again. He must be able to activate the inner eye. If his mind is placed in the land of living and dying, he will die in this land. He must therefore rise above existence and live in the continuity of his state of being. Study the plants as an example of this.

Know that there are those who will water the plants and care for them, so that they can rise above the soil while remaining rooted in it. And these caretakers are not worshipped by the plants, as the plants are aware of the food of light and appreciate all that is provided by the love of such. In love is immortality."

After the king said these things, the slaveholder and the slaves vanished from the face of the Earth as all things must. The king returned to his kingdom in the joy of being.

= Ka

Mantra: kah

Deity: Chiwashetkot-mat

Fear creates duality. This is why it is said that immortality will not descend upon those who hold fear in their hearts and minds.

Fear creates doubt. Fear creates worry. Fear creates anger. And the physical manifestation of fear is disease. Wherever there is fear, there is a lack of trust in the greater good, the Divine Mind.

Take up thy armor by making use of repetitive words that are sung when times of fear arise.

 = Ki

Mantra: Key

Deity: Hi-no-haya-hi-no-mikoto

There is no superiority between the yin and the yang, for they are both aspects of a cycle. Some refer to the yin and yang as objects, or some form of category. The yin and the yang are not objects but actions. One action leads to an experience where another action must be performed. We can say that the cycle of the yin and the yang is like the experiences of an embryo in its mother's womb, or a child during the early stages of life. All things are born from the void. When it rises from the yin it is called the yang.

Ame-no-Ukihashi

 = Ku

Mantra: Kuu

Deity: Shinatobe no mikoto

Since the yin aspect expresses itself in an experience as a component of yang symbolism, we learn that all things in our experience are also an extension of this truth. One can know the vital force of a person, and the principle they represent in the limits of humanity by simply listening to the words they speak. Communication is an unseen process regardless of the signs that are used in a particular experience. The mind behind the movements of speech is also invisible.

け = Ke

Mantra; Keh

Deity: Ichikishimahime-no-Mikoto

Understanding the voyage of Water is a ride upon
the waves of existence, an initiation into the
dimension of Love. Beware of those who speak
despairingly of life, as they know not its purpose.
And the realm of existence is like a child learning
how to swim, training the soul in the realms of
Love.

 = Ko

Mantra: Koh

Deity: Aya-hime-no-Mikoto

What is it that they really know? Those who live in
fear are not aware of the indignant blanket that
covers their lives. Every little thing is done to fix
this and that. Know that all problems are in fact
one problem, save that there is no problem at all.
These are the children of fear, a casualty to the
cultivation of Love, an evil vexation that is
unwilling to let go. Just remember that you are
within all things, and that which is feared has only
the power of illusion over you, as its true meaning
in known only to those who are initiated.

Abe no Seimei

There was once a woman who loved her husband dearly. Now the husband made his living as a traveling merchant and would often ride upon the sea to collect his goods from rich ports. During his time away from home, he would send a letter to his wife every day. Every day his wife would receive a letter from her husband.

One year, during the autumn season, a great war broke out while the husband was on journey by sea. The wife took to worry, as she did not receive a letter from her husband in eight days. Emotionally, she felt that her husband was fine, but that some sort of blockage had occurred. She decided to talk about this matter with a young onmyōji named Abe no Seimei. The young man had a strong reputation for his skill in the mysterious arts and had the ability to acquire knowledge in ways that were unbelievable to many.

The woman met Abe no Seimei in a garden that was north of a popular forest familiar to most of the townspeople. She explained the situation to the young onmyōji, even crying at his feet. Abe no Seimei felt compassion for the woman and listened intensely to everything she said.

After listening to the woman, the young onmyōji took to the forest near the garden and made the

woman promise that she would await his return.
Abe no Seimei remained in the forest for quite
some time. The woman waited patiently. They had
met in the garden early in the morning and it was
now nearing sunset. Abe no Seimei returned and
assured the woman that her husband was safe and
would return to her in three days.

Three days later the husband returned to his wife.
She was amazed at how accurate the words of Abe
no Seimei proved to be and decided to invite the
mystic over for a meal. The young onmyōji was
delighted to hear about the good news. When Abe
no Seimei arrived at the home of the man and
woman, the husband remarked that he had
conversed with the magician at a market just before
he set sail for home. The husband and wife were
fascinated by the power of the young onmyōji and
his ability to travel great distances with no
transport. Soon after these things occurred, the wife
gave birth to a male child that possessed an
extraordinary intelligence.

The husband and wife, being impressed by the
ability of Abe no Seimei, made arrangements for
their son to study with the onmyōji. Abe no Seimei
was delighted in the husband and wife's offer and
prepared a space for the teenager in his home. The
teenage boy worked with Abe no Seimei for quite
some time, but not in a way expected. Seimei had
assigned various household duties for the young
man to complete and spoke very little about any
esoteric knowledge. The son of the husband and

wife became frustrated in what he thought were menial tasks.

Now it came about that the queen of a distant land got to hear about the mysterious powers of Abe no Seimei and called him to her court for a special assignment. Accordingly, he left all of the affairs of his household under the charge of the young man. Alas, the young man was now able to study many of the books that Seimei had kept in his library.

And the son of the husband and wife would study the books of Abe no Seimei day and night. There were even some books that he did memorize. Although, the young man became knowledgeable of esoteric subjects and techniques, he could not perform any of the miraculous works that came so easily to his mentor. There was no improvement in the young man's magical ability no matter how many books he read. He soon became frustrated and resented his course of life.

Finally, Abe no Seimei returned back home. He was able to determine the young man's condition with a swift glance. The young man welcome Seimei back home, but questioned him in regard to the application of the information that he read in books. The son of the husband and wife angrily questioned Seimei about the methods that he had read about in the books and how to ascertain the mysterious power of legend. Seimei invited the lad out for a walk with him, walking to a forest nearby. The two began to journey through the woods of cedar and pine together. Seimei responded to the young man's questions in a calm voice:

"You stopped studying magic when you began reading the techniques found in books. There are a lot of ideas that can be conveyed in books, which are useful to the magician. Yet, these same ideas can be read and employed by an ordinary person with no success. This is usually the case. An ordinary man will make an esoteric truth complex. These things cannot be understood by the ordinary man because they are not written in the language of the ordinary man. He wrongfully assumes the meaning of what he has read for its literal value. The magician will read these same things and acquire a totally different meaning. The ordinary man will read even these words and begin to look for books that convey the magician's understanding of certain words. This too is a trap because the ordinary man is still looking for a literal meaning. A man's understanding can only be found in life. Since the life of the ordinary man and the magician are different, their interpretation of what they are reading will be different.

The ordinary man is seeking to impress others, find a solution to his problems, and curse people. The magician is simply seeking to serve what is good. Magic is very simple. Our experiences are created by the subconscious mind, which is called many names. There are many gods and goddesses that are merely symbols for the subconscious mind. Our desires and feelings are prayers to the subconscious mind. The subconscious mind will configure our experience based on the requests we make emotionally. It responds to such prayers regardless of our own moral standards. This is how experiences are born. We make prayers to become rich and our fears interfere with the progress of the experience unfolding.

This subconscious mind is a shared mind, not belonging to any one individual in particular. It is the government that all nations are ruled by. Our portion, our privilege to express ourselves in government, is how we interact with this communal subconscious mind. The subconscious mind responds to every thought, desire, and feeling that we have. And every thought, desire, and feeling fits somewhere in our past, present, or future experience. Every thought, desire, and feeling are the bricks of our experiences. The chores that you were given before my departure were designed to teach you this.

After witnessing this process, you must begin training your subconscious. You may not be able to control the influx of your thoughts and desires as they enter the subconscious mind, but you can recite certain words in times of need and repeat them as such. This is how we train the subconscious mind. What is invisible in our world is matter in the unseen realms, and what is invisible in the unseen realms is matter in this realm. A true martial artist understands these things. Recite these words when you are challenged by fear:

"I am surrounded by the light of Amaterasu Ohmikami. No negativity can penetrate my sphere of light."

When the vital energy is imbalanced, the subconscious mind will quickly give way to many thoughts, some benevolent and many that are poor in spirit. Therefore, it is important that the divine formulas of mythologies are used to cultivate this mysterious power. After the understanding of the mind has occurred, the practices often attributed to magic can be applied and studied."

Abe no Seimei and the young man returned from the forest. The young man began his chores again, which resulted in the experience of miraculous things. In the years that followed, the young man's reputation began to grow in the same manner as that of Abe no Seimei.

 = Sa

Mantra: Sah

Deity: Wakahirume-no-Mikoto

Know that in the world of humanity are many
lessons and teachings that are not spoken about.
This is a realm of learning. Some will create
theories that it can be more than what it is. Some of
their words will be encouraging. During other
times, their words will be the vehicle for evil spirits
to travel upon. Remember, that all their ideas and
theories are from the perspective of a creature who
sees the world through five senses.

$\cup$ = Shi

Mantra: Shee

Deity: Futsunushi-no-Kami

The senses of man define his function. Know that there are many more senses that man can acquire beyond the five. Surely, these senses will be learned in developing a relationship with aspects of the Self that possess such attributes, like the birds and the trees.

All that you see around you in creation are aspects of the mind of man collectively working as a single talisman.

す = Su

Mantra: Suu

Deity: Hoshi-no-Kami-Kakaseo

War occurs when something new is coming into this world. It is for this reason that we know of wars which are not violent. Some wars are emotional, others mental, and of course a great majority that are physical.

Know, also, that all of these wars are the result of invisible causes. In this case, all war is an unseen phenomenon, but still not a part of the Divine World.

せ = Se

Mantra: Say

Deity: Ihika

War is also a stage of development among manlike races existing in this world and in others. In the same manner that a child grows into a boy, and a boy into a man, so it is for the races of man.

War is to the race of man what puberty is to a young boy. Regardless of what advice the boy receives from the elders in his family, he must still go through puberty. After reaching puberty he enters a stage of knowing that could not be obtained without this experience.

= So

Mantra: Soh

Deity: Tsukiyomi-no-Mikoto

Everything that we experience is the result of some vow or an imagined work of fiction, resonating from the remote regions of our minds. It is important, therefore, that we get to know our internal talisman and how it manufactures what we experience.

Kongō of Kōya-no-Myōjin

Few engage the element of light. In ignorance they build their lives around rituals. Like men imitating the blind, deaf, and dumb, none of them can see or hear clearly. Is their magic also a source of binding intelligence in folly?

We know that the body is a temple. They pray in temples where evil spirits dwell. Look at their emotions they harbor day after day. Disciples of many disciplines are these, but still ignorant of the immortal way. How can one live forever if they are pressed against a haunting emotion? Do not be misled by their claims and deeds of magical showmanship. They do not understand what it truly means to be a worker of the mysterious art. A true magician is a warrior and a true warrior is a magician.

Emotions are vehicles entering the body through every portal of flesh. Some are from higher worlds and others from places that are dense and absent of compassion. Leave such things where they be. Step out of existence and take on the being of immortality. What more is perfection than a pure subconscious mind? Each and every mortal is deemed a fatality because of the impurities they host. What good is a cup of water if it contains a drop of poison in it? Still, they do not understand, whether right or wrong, the ill-emotions they harbor violate their own purity. Have you ever heard of purity in the dream? Salvation has no blemish. Immortality is that simple. Accept the garment of the spiritual warrior, cultivating and preserving love in the Divine Society.

They call those who follow the course of the stars lucky, as the stars themselves mark the path of karma. Some know how to bargain with the stars, making a good deal and profit from the treasures of luck. These things are good for the affairs of life and useful in obtaining earthly fortune. The study of planets and stars is the study of cause and effect, the law of karma, and the law of retribution, making calculations of times in order to find a favorable astral condition sent forth by the stars. Some will claim this science as their final resting place, but not the immortal.

Nevertheless, this world of celestial karmic law must be experienced, studied, and understood for it exists in a realm that is slightly above those who are not initiated and below the understanding of divine things. If the destiny of man is found in the fates called forth by the stars, then man himself is a machine. As the heat of the Sun is known and can be predicted, so too the experience of man. He exists in the earth without knowledge of where he came from. He is a Fool. The path is known by all, but followed by few.

Learning the Way requires work, not a formula. It is not found in magical books or grimoires. One must first understand that they are out of touch with their minds. During the time of sleep the light of distant stars assign to the mind a pattern of behavior fitting for its purpose.

There once lived a queen who ruled over a great celestial kingdom. She used her resources to provide the best means of living for all who resided in her nation, even the poorest of the poor ate better than the kings of legend.

The queen's beauty was matched by none living in the world. A star amidst a sea of crystal waters is how her sovereignty appeared among the nations. She had jet-black hair that grew past her ankles. People not only marveled at her beauty, but the wisdom she possessed. The queen was admired by the maidens, nurses, and mothers of the celestial kingdom. Men would often fantasize about being given her hand in marriage.

One day the queen decided to visit some of the impoverished lands, which her attendants had given a thorough report. She considered it a favorable opportunity to expand her kingdom and share in the joy of living. Although, her departure was celebrated for the fruitage it may yield, the queen felt doubt in the heart. "How could any place on earth ever equal the kingdom that I have established?"

Dark clouds hung in the skies over the impoverished land. The approaching queen entered the starving emotion alone. The winds brushed through the doors of the houses like ghosts. Dried tears of dust covered the streets where children once played. It was sunset and the reddened-sky was the only rose destined to be enjoyed.

The queen awoke. Surrounded by shadows, she stood confused. Dancing with sleep in the ignorance of music, save for those who watched her enter the city and knew not to let their eyes wander too far. A stranger never walks alone unless their heart is stricken with fear. The gates are opened by the glance of a trembling heart that knows not prayer or how to fight against a negative emotion.

Now the people of the impoverished land began to torment the queen. Fiercely, her sovereignty was disregarded in favor of lowly pursuits and pleasures. Freedom was enslaved, as it is with all people who live in poverty. Beaten and left on the side of the road, the queen was no longer the queen.

Soon after, the people of the impoverished land overran the kingdom of the queen, inflicting all sorts of demoralizing acts upon its citizens. These too, were forced to surrender their hopes of joy for the realities of evil.

The dark days of this time seemed infinite for a once enchanted kingdom. Evil forces posed as the creators of all who lived in fear. The queen was left for dead. The forces behind the sun took note of all the injustice that was occurring in the land. They felt pity for the misfortune that had befallen the queen and sent a refreshing wind to her rescue. With all her strength the queen crawled over to a nearby pond. The sun grew brighter the more her body stretched. Every step was a place of replenishment among the stars.

Finally, the queen reached the pond! She partook of the nourishment of her reflection. The more her strength was renewed, the brighter the sun shined. The flowers bloomed wherever the queen walked. All who were responsible for the evil that was done to the queen died of old age quickly. Not only did the queen extend her sovereignty to what was once an impoverished land now made fruitful, but her beauty had grown far beyond this world. The two lands became one and the joy it contained was insurmountable.

Where are all the magical incantations and fancy symbols in all of this? Before the queen went on her journey to an impoverished land she made profit off the movement of the planet and stars. This was the first magic, but not the complete initiation.

When the queen visited an impoverished land, she fell under the influence of negative emotions. The queen is the subconscious mind. Under the sway of depression and fear her experiences became unfavorable. There is no magical rite that can resolve a matter of the heart.

The voice behind the sun felt pity for the subconscious mind and came to its aid. This force, existing behind the sun, is the divine mind, what some call the mind of god. It is the place of spirit sitting upon the throne and the true sovereign ruler over the subconscious mind. Yet, the relationship between the two has been severed by misappropriated faith in marvelous things of no value and gossiping magicians, the conscious mind. Train the subconscious mind with the principles of divine law and the joy of creation will conform to your immortal request.

The queen was renewed by the refreshment of her very own reflection. When one can see that all experience is an outer manifestation of an inner experience the second initiation begins. In the same manner that the stars shine upon creation, we too shine upon our experience by the words we speak, our thoughts and inner ramblings.

Remember, Izanagi-no-Mikoto created the luminaries by the use of a white copper mirror. Amaterasu-Ohkami came out of the rock-cave after seeing her reflection in the mirror. *"The realm of Ninzuwu is said to be a place of mirrors above and below, side by side. It is a world of reflection, but the Ninzuwu walk about this Dream as upon solid ground."* How can one master their experience while ignoring the influences of the subconscious mind in the process of creation?

The names of the divine ones, the kami, are all mantras for emotions not known in the realm of existence. We know that a tree is not an astrologer, but if it is attacked by a ruthless insect; it will call

the predator of that insect by sending forth a
certain emotion. That emotion does not exist in the
realms of man. The flood of thoughts and desires
are not so easy to discern in the beginning. It is
necessary for the spiritual warrior to create a
watcher that will guard the subconscious mind
from attack. Our destiny is called forth by words.
Some are said mentally and others can be heard
clearly. Remember, words are the clothes of
emotions. Create then a prayer from the language,
held sacred among the Ninzuwu and arrange it in
an order to protect the subconscious mind from
disturbing mechanisms.

Each and every time a fearful emotion enters one's
thoughts, recite the statement of invisible
craftsmanship. During this time, one will
understand the meaning of life and its true
purpose. Those who seek superficial knowledge
will read about these things in a state of ecstasy
and soon forget the place where such practices
reside in their lives.

**"The light of Amaterasu Ohkami protects me. No
negativity can penetrate my divine state of being.
Aum-Aum-Phe-Hmu. I am a Ninzuwu, child of
the Kami, Amatsujin. Divine love fills my very
being, overcoming my obstacles and turning
enemies into friends. Hmu-Phe, Aum-Zhee-
Bnhu."**

Winds can be disturbing thoughts or a gentle
breeze when the sun is high. When the Land of

Mirrors takes hold of the mind, speak the word of thy Mother and let your light shine forth:

"The Divine Light within is beautiful and eternal. I will let it shine forth in every experience."

Do not be lazy in these undertakings! Some will refute the thoughts of fear and ponder those of adultery. Lust and anger will rob one of immortality like no other. This is why we say the law of karma must be studied, so that those who are sincere in their intentions do not deceive themselves.

It's not that difficult to understand. The light from the stars shine upon the subconscious mind and is then reflected in your experience. Take the attitude of the immortal and look upon such things as changes in the weather. Does a man have to be unhappy in the rain? It is the same with the light of the stars. Imagine their light as the rain. You can be happy once you see things as they are. And if the light of the stars enters the subconscious mind with a message, it is the same with stars themselves and how they speak to each other. Light is a form of communication. If there is no light, there are no words.

Ame-no-Ukihashi

た = Ta

Mantra: Tah

Deity: Shiho-tsuchi no Oji

Fights in Heaven are forfeited by throwing the first punch. Let not the mind curse an innocent man in silence. Bless your enemies, so as not to stain your own being with the impurity of another. Take no battle personally, but resolve such things in an egoless manner. Let the will of love be upon you.

ち = Chi

Mantra: Chee

Deity: Izanagi-no-Mikoto

Are not the clouds alive too? Clouds can decree a fatality by casting a thunderbolt. Clouds provide water for the benefit of plants and animals. Clouds appear dark when angry and white when life is bright. Only a Fool would believe that clouds have no consciousness. Clouds are the garments of an invisible dragon.

Ame-no-Ukihashi

 = Tsu

Mantra: Tsu

Deity: Kaminari-no-Ohkami

The clouds are the physical manifestation of an invisible force, like the body of man. In the study of this knowledge, one learns how to strengthen their own aura, as it is still the study of clouds.

= Te

Mantra: The

Deity: Sojobo-Tengu

Voices looking for dwelling places exist all around us. The wise one acknowledges this and strengthens his will. Few people have willpower, as few have actually taken the time to cultivate it.

と = To

Mantra: Toh

Deity: Tarobo-Tengu

Few wear crowns as great as the eye existing in its place. Stillness is an attribute cultivated by those who have disciplined the mind. So easily given to dark emotions they lose balance. Where is the mind in all of this? When the mind has reached a degree of tranquility, the body can be still.

な = Na

Mantra: Nah

Deity: Jirobo-Tengu

The focus placed on simple things helps one become strong in their craft. The supernatural world is a simple place filled with simple things. It is only made complex by a complex mind. When things become complicated, nothing gets done.

$$= Ni$$

Mantra: Nee

Deity: Sanjakubō-Tengu

Focus on simple things. The first task in this most-precious form of martial art is learning how to discern and move the different natures of invisible energies.

= Nu

Mantra: Nuu

Deity: Ryūhōbō-Tengu

One should spend a little time studying the clouds. If you study the clouds, you learn how to carry the clouds. If you can carry the clouds, you can change the weather of your experience.

 = Ne

Mantra: Ney

Deity: Buzenbō-Tengu

Is there any sense in the study of clouds? This, of course, is the question of the layman. They will forever live in doubt because doubt is faith in mortality. When we study the clouds, we can watch our emotions without getting involved with them.

$\mathcal{O}$ = No

Mantra: Noh

Deity: Amaterasu Ohmikami

Clouds have no attachments, but they fulfill their obligations with the utmost urgency. Beware of people who do not understand our ways and misinterpret the simple language to justify their ignorant lifestyles.

は = Ha

Mantra: Ha

Deity: Hōkibō-Tengu

All of life is the life of a cloud. The animals, man, plants, stars, and trees, all live the life of a cloud in their respective environments. Listen to the winds talk.

= Hi

Mantra; Hee

Deity: Myōgibō-Tengu

Your actions, emotional state, the words you speak and think, is the light that shines upon your experience, flavoring its weather, like the Sun shines upon Earth.

= Hu

Mantra: Huu

Deity: Sankibō-Tengu

It is an internal battle that one must face in the beginning. One day, when the initiate has finally gained a knowledge of themselves, they will see that every outer experience is a reflection of an internal thought or emotion, which was received by the light of a distant star. Your inner world is out in space.

= He

Mantra: Hay

Deity: Zenkibō-Tengu

Many stumble on the logic of others and the "right" ideas. Judge not the truth of words, but one's emotional state. This determines how positive and negative energies move. It is often said that a man can lead you into the Netherworld by telling a truth which puts you into a state of anger. It is this state of anger that will soon be your reality.

ほ = Ho

Mantra: Ho

Deity: Kōtenbō-Tengu

Take then the course of peace and use every transgression against you as a time to practice this sacred art. In this, you will learn how to defend yourself. When sad, invoke happiness. When angry, invoke peace.

 = Ma

Mantra: Ma

Deity: Tsukuba-hōin-Tengu

We create our own law by our thoughts and words.
It is necessary; therefore, that we condition our
bodies, as each organ has a mind of its own.

= Mi

Mantra: Mi

Deity: Daranibō-Tengu

The first sign of thy knowing comes with communication between the Sun and the Mind. After this, the hands learn how to speak with plants and trees.

= Mu

Mantra: Muu

Deity: Naigubu-Tengu

The subconscious mind can be found in a glass of
water. Spend some time staring into a glass of
water and let the particles show you a reflection of
your mind.

 = Me

Mantra: May

Deity: Sagamibō-Tengu

Preserving one's vital energy is like watching the snow fly in the wind. It takes practice. When certain laws are understood, this task can be accomplished with little restraint.

$$\text{Ƭ} = \text{Mo}$$

Mantra; Moh

Deity: Saburō-Tengu

Listen to the wind even when it is silent. Each and every day feel the air breathing. It will take practice, but once misunderstood you can hold a single snowflake in the blistering heat.

= Ya

Mantra: Yah

Deity: Ajari-Tengu

Guard yourself against anger. Sometimes negatives spirits will provoke thee to anger, and then feed off of the energy produced. The more you succumb to their designs, the longer these spirits will stick around you.

ゆ = Yu

Mantra: You

Deity: Yama-no-Shinbo

One must look beyond the present condition in the
world in order to see their true purpose in life.

$\int$ = Yo

Mantra: Yoh

Deity: Himekoso-no-Kami

Moving the body in stillness must be practiced
with the eyes covered, then without sound. Learn
from the sound that the rain makes before it hits
the ground. Effective kicking encompasses this
observation, as all kicking is a practice of decision-
making.

 = Ra

Mantra: Rah

Deity: Kukunochi-no-Kami

When thirsty, drink from the Air. When bathing, use Fire. When cooking, use Earth. When breathing, use Water. When living, use spirit.

= Ri

Mantra: Ree

Deity: Honotohatahimekochijihime-no-Mikoto

Every element, every form of natural phenomena has a life and a message to sing to all those who are living in existence.

= Ru

Mantra: Ruu

Deity: Iwanagahime-no-Mikoto

Wisdom begins with nothing. Knowing that you
have nothing to give to the universe, your objective
can only be achieved through hard work.

れ = Re

Mantra: Ray

Deity: Ame-no-Fukine-no-Kami

A wise person will develop a personal friendship with a plant or tree. They will take such a relationship seriously, as there is much to learn from those who can turn sunlight into food.

Talk to them about their reasons for making food. Talk to them about how they drink water. Ask them about their foundation and how they are able to stand up tall. This is the beginning of wisdom.

= Ro

Mantra: Roh

Deity: Uda-no-Sumisaka-no-Kami

Water is a mirror. Speak to a Body of Water during times of intensity. Listen to the words and the wisdom that the Body of Water has kept in expectation of your arrival.

You must find out a means of communication with the Water, use the parable that the Water represents.

わ = Wa

Mantra: Wah

Deity: Boshijin

Thy essence is in all things. Once the inner self has awakened, the technology of nature is unveiled. This knowledge, however, is not the aim of one's being. All is Self and that part which can see itself has the responsibility of taking care of the Self.

を = Wo

Mantra: Woh

Deity: Baku

Divine things are simple. Divine things are clean.
The Divine World is a space found in the world of
art. Art is a mediator for nature so that all can
know the intelligence of its tranquility.

$\mathcal{h}$ = N

Mantra: Unn

Deity: Ayaqox

It is the dance of exorcism that baptizes us in the waters of purity. Focus. Time is breath and the breath is motion. Think wisely!

Anointing of the Tengu

These are the instructions given to me by the
Magicians of the Secret Lands, also known as the
Tengu, concerning Ame-no-Murakumo-no-
Tsurugi, the Cloud-Gathering Sword of Heaven.

Those who follow these ways must be able to
invoke the Soul of Fire prayer, as set forth in the
Ivory Tablets of the Crow. They should be versed
in the Art of Ninzuwu. Each step of Ame-no-
Ukihashi is an incantation. It is for this reason that
you must invoke the mantra and visualize its letter
through each of the nine chakras, from Zhee to
Shki, and from Shki to Zhee, while holding the
body in the position described.

When one position of the Celestial Sword is
understood, move to the next. Practice all that you
have learned each day. Intentionally, there are no
instructions as to how you move from one position
to the next. How you move from one position to
the next is open to the understanding of the
practitioner, as it reveals where you are at in this
work.

There are some teachings that talk about techniques
of combat and how to use a certain movement
against an opponent. Know that such forms of
training are nothing more than prayers for conflict.
Imagining an opponent is a prayer, a special

request to create one. How then can one train the body in such matters?

Know that how one moves from one position to the next is the opponent. There is nothing to imagine. The movement itself is the opponent. We strive to move in stillness, like the voices of fallen raindrops before hitting the ground. Understand that in the movements of the body is found a manuscript of vertical writings, drawing down energy from Heaven. This is the way of Ame-no-Ukihashi-Do .

Each letter represents a physical position. It is a knowledge that is practiced by the Priests and Priestesses of Ninzuwu for the purpose of understanding the secret formulas written in the script of the woman's hand, hiragana.

Dancing is a form of purification. And it was known in times of antiquity that the priests and priestesses of the old rites were able to read ancient prayers written in hiragana and could interpret the sacred words as a martial dance, exorcizing the wandering spirits and bringing down energy from the stars.

Remember, that those who possess the title of a deity are not to be worshipped, but respected. It is against our creed to do otherwise. It is the same for any god or goddess who serves in the expansion of the Divine World. Yet, we pray to such as a form of communication and aid in service of the particular function and aspect of life they are given jurisdiction over. It is for this reason that one must inquire of the Snow Maiden themselves before acquiring the knowledge that can be gained from the martial dance listed herein.

Let it be known that before one can begin to practice Ame-no-Ukihashi , they must petition the Snow Maiden. This petition must be made by the use of a certain formula. The Priest and Priestess of Ninzuwu must invoke Ame-no-ukihashi-hime-no-Mikoto for nine days. Afterwards, they will witness an emissary from the race of Ame-no-Ukihashi-hime-no-Mikoto appear to them in dreams and by means of epiphany. It is this way as each of the Nine Dreams can only be entered by the call of the Watcher for that particular Dream.

Clap your hands three times, calling the name "Johuta" afterwards. The amount of times we clap is symbolic of the mind that is called and the name placed in each aspect of a particular part of the mind. Perform the Opening of the Sea. Make the Soul of Fire Prayer. Invoke the Shamuzi. Recite "Johuta" three times then clap three more times. Perform these things in respects to the Ancient One.

After these things have occurred, one must bow twice. Clap twice. Bow once. In this case, the amount of times one takes a bow is in respect to the forces of the three planes of existence, physical, astral, and finally the Divine World.

Recite the Prayer of Heaven, the Amatsu Norito, three times. Invoke the mantra of Amaterasu

Ohmikami by reciting her name nine times. Now invoke the Snow Maiden by this formula:

"Ame-no-Ukihashi-hime-no-Mikoto mamori tamae sakihae tamae"

These words should be said once for each of the nine chakras, from Zhee to Shki. After reaching Shki, the mantra should be recited in an ascending path from Shki to Zhee. During this empowerment, one must hold the Star of Ame-no-ukihashi-hime-no-Mikoto in each chakra, for both descending and ascending motions.

The Star of Ame-no-ukihashi-hime-no-Mikoto

Express your gratitude to the Snow Maiden. She will soon come to you in dreams and teach you the deeper things of the Way.

After you have invoked the Snow Maiden, you must perform the Hi Fu Mi three times. This will open the heart and mind to the ways of Heaven.

HI-FU-MI-YO-I-MU-NA-YA-KO-TO
MO-CHI-RO-RA-NE-SHI-KI
RU-YU-I-TSU-WA-NU-SO
O-TA-HA-KU-ME-KA-U-O-E-NI
SA-RI-HE-TE-NO-MA-SU-A-SE-HE-HO-RE-KE

The Priest and the Priestess should now make use
of an Iyasaka formula used only by the Ninzuwu. It
should be offered once and to the ancestors of our
sacred tradition:

Iyasaka Prayer

Kuni-no-tokotachi-no-Mikoto, Iyasaka Iyasaka,
Iyasaka

Kuni-no-satsuchi-no-Mikoto, Iyasaka Iyasaka,
Iyasaka

Toyo-kumo-nu-no-Mikoto, Iyasaka Iyasaka,
Iyasaka

Uhijini-no-Mikoto, Suhijini-no-Mikoto, Iyasaka
Iyasaka, Iyasaka

Otonoji-no-Mikoto, Otomabe-no-Mikoto, Iyasaka
Iyasaka, Iyasaka

Omo-Daru-no-Mikoto, Kashiko-ne-no-Mikoto,
Iyasaka Iyasaka, Iyasaka

Prayer of Heaven

Taka ama hari ni Kamu zumari masu Kamurogi
Kamuromi no Mikoto moshite
Sumemi oya Kamu Izanagi no Ohkami Tsukushi
no Himuka no Tachibana no
Odo no Awagigahara ni Misogi harae tamaishi
Toki ne are maseru
Harae do no Ohkami tachi Moromoro no Maga
goto Tsumi kegare-o
Harae tamae Kiyome tamae to Maosu kotono
Yoshi-o
Amatsu kami Kunitsu kami Yao yorozu no Kami
tachi tomo ni Kikoshi mese to
Kashi komi Kashi komi mo mao su

Close the empowerment by stating "Kan-nagara
tamachi ha-e mase" three times. Two bows, two
claps, and one bow. After the empowerment is
performed for nine days one can return to the
practices of the priesthood. The Star of Ame-no-
ukihashi-hime-no-Mikoto should be remembered
during the new moon of each month.

Wandering Spirits

Know that the Priests and Priestesses of the Art of
Ninzuwu must walk through the world without
fear. Yet, this honor is not given to ordinary man,
as one can only reap what they have worked for.

The Magicians of the Unseen Lands know well the
mechanisms of the wandering spirits and have
passed this knowledge down to us. Remember that
nothing ever changes in the worlds held below the
fourth dimension, same appearance made new in
the vestibule of time.

In the days of old, the prophets called the ghetto
and the streets, the Netherworld. When the people
say "they have love for the streets," then you know
their god well. What more is a religion than the
ways and actions of a man and not what he thinks
of himself as being?

Here are a few things for those who are faithful in
the work to observe wherever they may travel, so
as to leave the door of the Netherworld closed.

The overuse of foul words is the first sign of a
wandering spirit's attachment to an individual's
aura. While there are situations where aggressive
words can act as a medium for blocking pain, evil
versus evil if you will. However, the excessive use
of vulgar language should be avoided.

Those who know the Dream of Ninzuwu are well
aware that the words we speak foretell the weather
of our experience. The abundant use of abusive
language reveals signs of an approaching storm or
conflict, the internal dark clouds and thunder.
Wandering spirits exist on the plains of lower
vibrations and they forever seek to pull elements of
the physical realm into a lower frequency so they
can have access to what is desired.

Violent actions are usually preceded by either
internal or external abusive speech, for it is a form
of violence unto its own. People who make it a
priority to use such words, live a life that is void of
happiness. Cursing words send out a vibration that
will return to its sender without fail.

Poverty breeds poverty. When you see a group of
men standing in front of a marketplace, know that
this is a sign of a gathering place for wandering
spirits in that village. Any money spent in such
places breeds poverty because the energy around
such places does not facilitate growth, but an
addiction to what is evil. It should be remembered
that money is a magical talisman, full of symbols,
and each government is under charge to create
such a document for the purpose of the ruling
genie presiding over that country.

Men who spend their time constantly standing in
front of the marketplace have no foundation in life.
They are under the influence of a wandering spirit
of a deceased homeless person. Both the man who

loiters in front of a store and the mother who is constantly sending her children to such markets, are both afflicted by the spirit of a binbogami. A binbogami, the kami of poverty, usually appears as a skinny old man with uchiwa in his hand.

The binbogami is also symbolic of someone who lives in a poor environment, but dresses in expensive clothes and obtains a lot of flashy possessions, for these are the true signs of poverty. It is the Way of Heaven and Earth that one cares for their environment first. Benevolent spirits cannot inhabit a dirty place. A neighborhood that is dirty is a stool of bad luck.

Poverty is not a financial matter, but an emotional condition. If a person follows the Way of Heaven and Earth they can enjoy the same experiences as the richest people in the world. Wealth is also an emotional state, a perspective in relationship to one's purpose in life and that of the universe. There are many rich people in the world who are not wealthy and live a troubled life.

Homelessness has its rules, as it is close to the spirit realm, true homelessness. It is said that if you pass a homeless person who rambles in their speech, but gives you some timely advice in their ecstatic state and able to answer a question about something in your life, give them money or a meal. If what they are rambling about, however, has no value to you, then such a donation is optional.

Beware of the things that intoxicate the mind and the body. Many medicine men of the field used these substances as a method for contacting the spirit world. The addiction to such things was created by gangster spirits.

Gangster spirits are a group of negative energies that often prey upon humankind. They encourage addiction so they can enter the phenomenal world through the empty mind of the person who is in the clouds. Upon entering the physical plane they seek ways and opportunities to create havoc. Sometimes they will cause an earthquake, killing thousands. Other times, they will possess the mind of a killer. Gangster spirits are very cunning for they will create philosophies among the masses that will make it easier for them to enter this world, the street life.

The streets are filled with disincarnate spirits. Only a fool can have love for the streets as the streets does not care for its own. It is ruled by wandering spirits who were murdered in the past and are still in pain. It is ruled by the Goryo.

Acts of sexual perversion are considered acts of violence in the spiritual world. Pornography is ruled by the disincarnate spirits of prostitutes who were murdered or committed suicide. While it may appear to be a glamorous and pleasurable business for some, many of its actors and actresses live short lives. This form of entertainment breeds depression for both the viewer and the actress.

These things are ruled by Yomotsu-shikome, who weaken the eyes and the kidneys.

Know that there is fear in the conspiracy theory, and fear is faith in evil instead of good. Nothing grows out of fear. The conspiracy theory is based on logic not the internal cultivation of varying emotional states, which is the great work. Conspiracy theories are one of the greatest forms of advertisement used by the certain factions of political world in order to create a disenchanted population that is more prone to commit crime, thereby fulfilling the quota forecasted by rich people who invest in prison building. The conspiracy theory is the conspiracy theory.

Be watchful of those who make predictions of the future. Avoid the use of their services if at all possible. A charlatan, who is ruled by wandering spirits, will never advise you simply on the good. Benevolent energies seeking to improve life overall may warn of calamity, but they will always provide means to relieve such. Often times, a person will ignorantly invite wandering spirits into their lives at the advice of a charlatan. The result is that these same energies, which often pose as gods and goddesses, will create problems in a person's life so that they themselves can be petitioned to relieve what they caused.

These are just a few things that the wandering spirits preside over. Your understanding of such things will increase the stronger you become. Be fearless!

Story of the Sword of Ninzuwu

During the times of the great emperors, Susanoo-
no-Mikoto went down and came to the head-
waters of the River Ye, in the province of Aki.
There the Lord Ashinazutenadzu resided by the
River Ye along with his wife who is called Inada-
no-Miyanushi-Susa-no-yatsumimi. Now the Lord
Ashinazutenadzu's wife, Inada-no-Miyanushi-
Susa-no-yatsumimi was pregnant with child, but
the husband and wife grieved. They spoke to Lord
Susanoo, saying: "Though we have had many
children born to us, whenever one is born, an *eight-
forked serpent* comes and devours the child, and we
have not been able to save any of our children. We
are about to have another child and we fear that
our child will be devoured like the others. This is
why we grieve."

Lord Susanoo listened intently to the husband and
wife's concern. He instructed the husband and
wife, saying: "Take the fruit of all kinds, and brew
from it eight jars of sake, and I will kill the serpent
for you.' The husband and wife followed Lord
Susanoo's instructions and prepared the sake.
When the time came for the child to be born, the
serpent came to the door and was about to devour
the child. But Lord Susanoo addressed the serpent,
saying: "You are an awesome force indeed! Can I
dare to neglect to feed thee?" Lord Susanoo took
the eight jars of sake and poured one into each of
the serpent's mouths. The serpent drank it and fell

asleep. Lord Susanoo then took out his sword and slew the serpent. When he tried to sever the serpent's tail, Lord Susanoo noticed that his sword was slightly notched. He split the tail open and examined it, and found that there was a sword inside the serpent's tail. This sword is called Kusanagi But, the Ninzuwu originally named the sword, Ame-no-Murakumo-no-Tsurugi, which means "Sword of the Gathering Clouds of Heaven." Lord Susanoo gave the sword to Amaterasu Omikami as a sign of repentance.

Ame-no-Ukihashi-hime-no-Mikoto

This is the Revelation of Ame-no-Ukihashi-hime-no-Mikoto. These words are written in the manner of dreams, as it was revealed to the Ninzuwu of Old, the priesthood called Ninigi-no-Mikoto, by the mouth of the one that walks upon the winds of time.

Know that these words are a blessing for those who have entered and possess an accurate knowledge of the Nine Dreams. Faithfully, they speak with the trees of nature and many of the marvelous minds from which the Divine World holds intercourse with.

During the days of old, lived a certain man named Jofuku, also known as Xifu in foreign lands. Jofuku was skilled in the magical arts and brought great delight to Emperor Shikoutei, under which he served.

Now it came about that Emperor Shikoutei, after observing the cycles of life and death for some time, became anxious over the dead, crying: "I must find a means of overcoming death? Why does man suffer such a horrible fate?"

The wife of Emperor Shikoutei was a beautiful maiden. She spoke to her husband about the lotus of eternal life, saying: "In ancient times, there lived

a woman named Ame-no-Ukihashi-hime-no-
Mikoto of the Ninzuwu, a Yuki-onna, who knows
the immortal formula. None dare confront the
brilliance of her aura. She has been living since the
kami-yo. Some say, Ame-no-Ukihashi-hime-no-
Mikoto resides in the mountain of Horai on the sea
to the east. You must dispatch Jofuku at once!"

Now the emperor found wisdom in the words of
his wife and dispatched Jofuku immediately, along
with the company of armed guards, fellow
craftsmen, and women who knew the art of sowing
and weaving. For twenty-one days Jofuku and his
attendants journeyed until they arrived at the base
of Mount Horai.

Jofuku went into trance and saw a woman seated
upon a throne in the clouds. Her was bright as the
Sun. After witnessing these things, Jofuku decided
to climb the mountain alone, informing only the
guards of his departure. The guards promised the
magician that they would keep silent about his
journey.

Jofuku reached the top of the mountain and a very
amazing sight appeared before him. It was an
opening between the dimensions. The magician
stood in fear as he saw a house made out of the
four seasons. Staring at the northern side of the
house was like looking into winter. Staring at the
eastern side of the house was like looking into
spring. Staring at the southern side of the house
was like looking into summer. Staring at the

western side of the house was like looking into autumn.

The house sat on a lawn of fire and ice. Jofuku could see a luminous figure, with the shape of a woman, dancing in the doorway of the house. Suddenly, there was a force that moved the magician's body beyond his own control. He found himself walking across the lawn of fire and ice with ease. The closer Jofuku came to the doorway of the house, the clearer the image of the woman became. She was a beautiful maiden with long black hair and a soft radiant complexion. Her eyes were like a cat's stare.

Now before this time, only those who lived in the mountains practiced Ninzuwu, as they knew the formula of immortality. Jofuku, now standing directly in front of the luminous spirit-woman that danced in the doorway, heard a question in his mind. "What are you doing here? What is it that you desire of Ame-no-Ukihashi-hime-no-Mikoto?"

The magician became calm after hearing the spirit's name, thinking the name of the spirit may give him control over it. He went on to explain the reason for his visit, saying: "I am Jofuku sent by my superiors in search of the lotus flower of immortality. In my land, I am a great magician, who has studied all the alchemical sciences of man."

Now the spirit-woman, named Ame-no-Ukihashi-hime-no-Mikoto, replied to the magician, saying: "You have studied the stupid things of man, like so many other magicians in your civilization. Did the idea of climbing this mountain come from your lower or higher self? How many actions do you take in life knowing the answer to this question each and every time?"

Ame-no-Ukihashi-hime-no-Mikoto entered the mind of Jofuku and brought him to a peaceful place. In the mind of Jofuku, Ame-no-Ukihashi-hime-no-Mikoto did take up residence and the magician had awakened in consciousness at the palace of the Ninzuwu. Jofuku sat at a long table, which was filled with every kind of food that could be imagined.

"I never ask myself those questions because time doesn't exist. I have read many of the ancient scrolls written by those who practiced the mysterious arts, since times of remote antiquity, and these books state that time is an illusion." Jofuku replied.

Ame-no-Ukihashi-hime-no-Mikoto's faced became brighter, shining like a day of newly-fallen snow. After listening to the words of Jofuku, she stated: "Indeed you are a fool, knowledgeable only in the way of reading books! Time is motion, and whatever moves is under the law of time and space. Time is an illusion just as much as this world is an illusion.

I see in your memory that you were sent here by an emperor. If time didn't exist, the journey you took to get here wouldn't exist also. When the magicians of old referred to the illusion of time, it was in regard to the world of the subconscious mind.

The subconscious mind controls most of what we say and do. It creates the experiences that we enjoy and dislike. The world that you live in is a shadow of the subconscious mind. The subconscious mind is the real world. Time in the subconscious mind does not exist. In the subconscious mind, there is no time between one desire and the next, between one thought and the next. At least from our perspective in this world of phenomena. The meaning of time changes in each and every world.

Think of how our bodies, standing in the light of the Sun, creates a visible shadow. Look at how all the actions of the shadow are created by the physical body in the light of the Sun. The shadow is our phenomenal world. The physical body in the light of the Sun is our subconscious mind. The Sun is the Divine World. Time is different for each realm from the perspective of the one underneath it.

The reason why the magicians of old wrote that time is an illusion was to awaken the mind of the one who knew the Way, not for those who stood outside the Way. The worker of the mysterious arts knows the power of the subconscious mind and how to use it. Our desires and thoughts make impressions on the subconscious mind, which begins to configure reality according to our desires. Our words, however, can regulate such things. Our words are our watcher.

In the beginning it is not easy to control our desires, our thoughts. We can, however, control our words. Our words act in the same manner as a gardener tilling the soil. If we speak in phrases that denote time, like, "I will," or, "I was," it makes little sense to the hidden mind. Such statements are like a man getting attacked by an army and tries to defend himself by talking about what he was or what he is going to be. The subconscious mind responds immediately to statements made in the moment. "I am victorious" is just one example of this."

And Jofuku listened intently to the words of Ame-no-Ukihashi-hime-no-Mikoto. After saying these things Ame-no-Ukihashi-hime-no-Mikoto cast another dream upon the mind of Jofuku. The magician then saw himself in a world of great machinery. It was nothing he had ever seen before, in regards to a world of man. The people of this world lived in tall structures and worked, not with nature, but held faith in the machines they designed. Instead of living in nature, man would visit nature in its imprisoned state.

Jofuku was astonished to see people eating food out of packages, which were designed by the machines. Men were able to kill men with their iron tools and would entertain themselves by watching the death of other human beings. Day and night the people of this civilization worked to become like the slave owners who held them captive. The people even formed religions around the slave owner's mind and began saying: "Life needs the sacrifice of death in order to forgive. This world is all about money. Why should we care for our family and our neighbors?" After seeing these things, Jofuku let out a great cry, saying: "What is this?"

A mouth appeared in the clouds and the voice of Ame-no-Ukihashi-hime-no-Mikoto spoke to Jofuku, saying: "This is the world in time, a world of the five senses. They call it logic. It poses as something new, an advanced stage of consciousness to the people living in this time. Logic is nothing more than a religion. It teaches its followers that only what can be confirmed by the five senses is real. This is the religion of logic."

Now Jofuku, listened to the voice of Ame-no-Ukihashi-hime-no-Mikoto, but could not understand the meaning of her words and so he asked: "How is logic a religion?" Then the voice of Ame-no-Ukihashi-hime-no-Mikoto began to speak, saying: "Our senses dictate what we eat and how we reproduce, but these things are only true for the purpose we hold. The senses of a man and the senses of a tree are different, but one is not the truth for the other. Each is true for the purpose for which it was designed.

A tree does not see the world as a man does. Yet, its perception is accurate, in some ways, even more than the senses of man. It can also be said that there are trees, which possess an intelligence that is superior to man. The senses of a tree allow it to

communicate with the Sun and provide food for
both animals and human beings. It even affects the
quality of the air we breathe. The senses of man
only reveal a portion of a reality that is allotted to
man. It is not the truth, as logic would like us to
believe.

The people of this civilization have built machines
to reinforce their belief in the five senses. They
have misled themselves into believing that their
ignorant faith of logic makes them wiser than
civilizations that have existed before this time. The
man of this era is the result of the stupidity of the
nations that existed prior, for his narcissistic
mentality believes that only those things which
possess the same senses as he does, is intelligent.
When the opposite side of this thinking is true. The
consciousness of man is possessed by more than
just human beings with different sensory
perception."

After Ame-no-Ukihashi-hime-no-Mikoto spoke the
wise words, the sky opened up. Jofuku looked up
and beheld the glory of this world viewed from
senses other than those possessed by ordinary man.
Then appeared a hand in the sky of enormous size,
like that of a small island. The hand extended its
reach to Jofuku and swallowed the magician up in
its grasp.

Jofuku opened his eyes gradually after being
awakened by the bark of a dog. The sun was rising
and the morning dew held a fragrance that

reminded the magician of his youth and growing up along the countryside.

The magician saw that he was on top of the same mountain that he climb only a day ago. Ame-no-Ukihashi-hime-no-Mikoto appeared to him as a simple maidservant. "How did you come upon this knowledge?" Jofuku asked. "The things I have seen today are nothing like anything that I have ever witnessed before."

"These things have always been a part of being here." Ame-no-Ukihashi-hime-no-Mikoto replied, while stirring the stew that she was preparing for Jofuku. She then took a bowl and filled it up with the stew, giving a portion of the stew to the magician. Ame-no-Ukihashi-hime-no-Mikoto eyes began to glow like a cat. She continued:

"Many of the workers of the mysterious arts find themselves remaining in the karmic world, the world of cause and effect, the world of retribution. The limit of their understanding is in the planets and stars, the light of which casts fates on the subconscious mind during sleep. Magicians of this sort will bargain with these celestial powers for a means of good luck and such is the law in the phenomenal world.

The way of the planet and stars is the law of karma and of retribution. When it is winter in one part of the Earth, it is summer in another part. It is what it is, so too with the laws of karma. It is nothing personal. When someone is enjoying a good fortune on one side of an experience, another person is suffering from ill-luck. When a planet moves into a certain position, it will be favorable for some and unfortunate for others, simply because we are all born at different times. From the perspective of the starry world, we are all living on different earths.

Initiation into the world of karma is a necessary thing, for it teaches us the laws of this world and the influences that people are under. Once this has been learned and internalized, the door may open up to the higher worlds. This transition is not a logical one, and for an unworthy magician this course will make no sense to him at all. One must be pure in heart in order to understand such things and out of this perspective can things of this nature be seen.

There is a mind that is higher than the subconscious mind. It cares nothing for an incantation or a ritual. Yet, it is much more powerful than the magic of the mind. This is the dimension of love and love is able to move the real world, the subconscious mind, in a way that appears to be miraculous to the ordinary man.

The names of the Kami and the Ninzuwu are words that invoke a fourth-dimensional consciousness into our lives. This fourth-dimension is the subconscious mind. The magician, who knows the way of perfect ideas, soon learns that the spirit seated on the throne has reign over the subconscious mind. Many can perform spells, cure diseases, and make a poor man rich, but very few of these workers understand the way of immortality."

After Ame-no-Ukihashi-hime-no-Mikoto spoke to Jofuku, she then revealed the mind of the Ninzuwu to the magician in the form of a crow. Henceforth, Jofuku understood the wisdom of Ame-no-Ukihashi-hime-no-Mikoto and began the work of teaching and initiating those of his company in the Sacred Rites of the Nine Dreams.

And the reputation of Jofuku began to spread amongst those living in the surrounding nations. Some began to pay tribute to him in the manner of an emperor. Jofuku was the first to teach the Art of Ninzuwu to those living outside the mountains.

Appendix A: What Is Shinto?

Shinto is often described as the indigenous faith of the Japanese people. It is probably more correct to define Shinto as being the indigenous faith of the human race that has been preserved by the Japanese people.

Different than many religions of the world, Shinto has no founder and no body of sacred writings which its adherents must follow, and this aspect of Shinto reveals that it was the primordial faith of the human race. The idea of a religion having a founder and its practitioners must follow a set of "sacred" writings can only be defined as someone from an advanced civilization sharing its culture with an uncivilized people. Think about it for a second. Although religious mythology throughout the world may vary, there is one point that is consistent among these; all of the world's "prophets" that carried a "divine message" had to deliver such to an uncivilized people, or a nation that fell in disaccord with the way of heaven and earth.

Shinto reveals there was a time when man held the standard of its creator, following the ways of heaven and earth. It was a time of innocence, though concerns over the basic human needs and survival were always prominent in the mind of man from his beginning.

While it may be difficult for some to imagine the life of the human race during a time of such innocence, if we were to reflect on the basic aspects of life that preoccupied man during times of remote antiquity, the vision is easy to capture. Families worked as a unit to acquire food, shelter, and clothing. In such an environment, life was simple and egoless.

It was in this egoless state that the clarity of man's role in the universal scheme of things was easily seen. Human existence could not be possible if nature did not provide man with food, sustenance, and shelter. Based on such, it is evident that man was dependent on its primary parents, the Earth, the Sun, and other aspects of nature that life, and its sustaining qualities were all made possible. Following the *way of the gods*, is following the science of life. It was during the 6th century A.D., after Mahayana Buddhism had taken root in Japan, that this science of life was called Shinto in effort to distinguish this primordial faith from foreign spiritual practices that were gaining popularity in the Land of the Rising Sun.

The term Shinto is composed of two kanji, *"shin"* meaning *divine, gods, or spirits*, known as Kami, and *"to"* meaning *path of study, the way*, a derivative of the Chinese term *tao. The term Shinto was used to describe the practices of the indigenous people of Japan, and in some ways these practices resembled many of the rites practiced by Taoists who entered Japan from China. Taoism is another faith that borrowed much from the nature cults existing in China.* The Encyclopedia of

World Environmental History, Volume 3, by
Shepard Krech, states the following on page 1111:

"Many scholars now believe that Japanese
actually borrowed the word "Shinto" from an
eighth-century Chinese word for Taoism...In the
eighth century, the Yamato state that Taoist
priests travel to Japan from China, and in time the
entire Japanese conception of empire and even
the cult of emperors themselves took on a Taoist
flavor. Nonetheless, early Japanese probably did
not identify, isolate, and categorize Shinto as
their "religion." Rather, for a people who lived
close to nature on a wild and mountAinuus
archipelago, Shinto probably constituted
everything they knew and sought to know about
the natural world."

Krech's observation confirms points presented in
our discussion. First, the indigenous practices that
relate to the nature cults of Japan, which were
later called Shinto, were not viewed as a
"religion" in the modern sense of the term, but
was in fact the science of life. Secondly, we learn
that *"Shinto probably constituted everything they
knew and sought to know about the natural
world."*

Different than present-day opinions, it is modern
man who has regressed during recent times and
become primitive in his thinking. He is now a
terror to the very thing that sustains his life,
nature. His ego dictates that he is superior to the
very thing he needs to survive. The ego of modern
man has led him to categorize those who followed

the *ways of the gods* as primitive. It is a sad state of affairs indeed, for he has lost his way and does not know how to communicate with the world around him, something that every living creature in nature can do. It is interesting to note that even in the insect world, there is a relationship between creatures of different kinds, plant life, and the heavenly bodies. Unfortunately, the ego of modern man has made it appear that the reverse is true, where the nature cults of old were not advanced in their knowledge and were primitive in thinking.

While the ego of modern man has led to the massive destruction of Earth's ecological system, he attempts to reinforce his egotistical views on the world by exalting the religions of the handicapped. A religion whose adherents believe in morbid concepts, like the creator of our entire universe requires a human sacrifice to forgive man, and still be considered a *god of love*. Another hypocritical belief is that the creator of our entire universe would actually command one nation to go out and kill every man, woman, and child, of an opposing nation in order to acquire some land. It is in the propagation of these so-called religious ideas that we find the plights of an egotistical sociopath accepted as the actions of an intelligent being. After establishing a spirit of disillusionment by spreading such morbid propaganda around the world, modern man then attempted to invalidate his own point of origin in an effort to appear superior. Today, we find this hypocrisy has finally spread to areas of academia as seen in the modern definition of Shinto itself.

Many Western sources have implied that Shinto began around 700 A.D. This is a ridiculous claim since we know that Shinto has no founder or sacred body of scriptures. If Shinto has no founder how can it be given a said date of origin? Efforts such as these clearly illustrate how propagators of various morbid systems of spirituality try to make their degrading theological views actual fact. It is a very sad thing indeed.

Shinto is the science of life. The indigenous people of Japan knew it as such, and incorporated in it are all aspects of life, including philosophy, religion, and science. Shinto is not a belief system, but the life you lead. There are many Japanese people who view religion as a system of control, or for the emotionally handicapped. It is due to such that many Japanese people will say they are atheists. This view does not make them less spiritual in their approach to life. But systems that appear separate from life are viewed as schemes to rob the spiritually malnourished. The fact that "Shinto" itself is not a religion, but a way of life, can be seen in its most scientific aspect, namely, the Kami.

Appendix B: The Kami

The heart of Shinto, or Japanese spirituality, cannot be captured if one lacks an understanding of the Kami. Kami is usually defined in the West, as the Japanese word for effigy, a principle and any supernatural being. While many attempts have been made by Western scholars to define the term *Kami*, it would be a grave error to compare such to the gods and spirits of Biblical mythology. This is not to say that it is wrong to define the term *kami* as gods, spirits, and sentient beings, but this perspective is quite different than how Christians revere Jesus Christ.

The term *kami* consist of two parts, *ka* meaning fire, and *mi* meaning water. Therefore, an accurate description of the term kami would be the alchemy of fire and water. Still, for the Western mind, and those outside the view of ancient Japanese thought, this in itself may not be clear definition.

The fire referred to in our discussion so far, is the radiating energy over a particular environment. For example, the appearance of a rose garden triggers a certain amount of emotional influence upon all other objects in that same environment. This radiating emotional energy is the *ka* or fire. The ka of an object can be suppressed or expanded based on the atmosphere it exists in. While the radiating

force of a rose garden may thrive in a certain
atmosphere, like a sunny day in the month of June,
its influence would not be as strong during
wintertime. The different atmospheric conditions
play a large part in how much emotional energy
any given object can radiate. These atmospheric
conditions, or atmosphere, are symbolic of water or
mi. In a previous work entitled, *The Dark Knight of
Nyarlathotep*, we find the following under the
chapter *True Religion*:

"In the so-called modern world, terms like
polytheism seem to denote some sort of primitive
form of spirituality, when in fact, it was a
synthesis of how to define the subtle energy that
permeates throughout all objects and animates all
living things. So in ancient times, a body of water,
or an ocean, was considered to be a deity. Now
the fact that this ocean was considered to be a
deity should not be interpreted in the same
manner of how Christians worship Jesus, but as a
force of influence upon the environment. Other
objects of nature were also deified based on their
influence over the environment. These forces
were scientifically categorized based on how
much subtle energy they emitted into the
atmosphere and their influence on objects in the
surrounding area, which led to its placement in
the hierarchy of natural forces.

These forces were recorded in history as pagan
gods, making it easy for the layman to understand
them. These forces were also measured by the
influence they had on the emotional constitution

of animals and humans. Since man possessed an abundance of subtle, or life-force energy, he could use this energy to alter the influence of a powerful force by calling its name (vibrational formulae) and speaking to the energy that resonated behind the said object, be it animal, plant, or star. Speech is vibration, and how words and letters are put together affect other objects vibrating on a subtle level. The enunciation of the names of these forces matched their vibrational level, and in turn they responded in favor of man. The subtle force that is radiated by all animated life was known as fire, and the atmosphere was considered to be water."

Understanding the Kami from this perspective redefines Japanese spirituality for the Western mind. A Japanese deity that rules over the auto industry is not some pagan god, but a force of influence upon the modern world. The force that is responsible for automotive technology can be called upon once it is given a name. Calling upon this name will allow Japanese automotive engineers access to the same ideas that led to the invention of the automobile. Thus, after entreating the *emotional energy* or *kami* that is behind the engineering, manufacturing, and technology of the automotive industry, they will be given the knowledge to advance such.

Within Shinto lies the understanding of how to manage and curb the emotional energy, the ki that radiates from objects, thoughts, and ideas in one's experience, for the personal benefit of all, or that of a village, or the nation at large. This way of thinking was an inherent result of the hunter-gatherer culture of ancient Japan. In pre-historic Japan, it was important for ancient man to have a working relationship with the environment that he lived in. It was due to this relationship with nature that men learned how to detect the emotional energy found in all objects and procure such to the benefit of his people. This "technology" enabled prehistoric man with the ability of curbing disastrous weather conditions, flooding, and etc.

Through a loving, reverential relationship with his environment, early man found that the vibration of his words expressed in certain emotional states, the fire, motivated a favorable response from the world around him. In a classic work on the topic of Shinto, by Sokyo Ono entitled, *Shinto: The Kami Way*, the author defines the Kami as follows:

"Among the objects or phenomena designated from ancient times as kami are the qualities of growth, fertility, production; natural phenomena, such as wind and thunder; natural objects, such as the sun, mountains, rivers, trees, and rocks; some animals; and ancestral spirits. In the last-named category are the spirits of the Imperial ancestors, the ancestors of noble families, and in a sense all ancestral spirits. Also regarded as kami are the guardian spirits of the land, occupations, and skills; the spirits of national heroes, men of outstanding deeds and virtues, and those who have contributed to civilization, culture, and

human welfare; those who have died for the state or community; and the pitiable dead. Not only spirits superior to man, but even some that are regarded as pitiable and weak have nonetheless been considered to be kami."

After having considered the true meaning of the Kami, Ono's statement can be easily conceptualized, as they all refer to forces of emotional influence. It is with this perspective that we begin to understand Shinto not as a religion, but as the science of life; a science that explains how energy is exchanged between objects existing in the same environment. We also become aware that the rituals conducted in Shinto is a way to curtail these energies to suit ones' needs and strengthen their ancestral line.

The Esoteric Black Dragon Society

1. The Esoteric Black Dragon Society appreciates the sacred technology of Shinto and Yi Jing Sorcery as a gift from the source of all things, which is to be used for the spiritual advancement of humanity and to cultivate the world and the individual. The use of such technology for purposes of self-glorification is strictly forbidden.

2. The term "god" should not be associated with the Creator, nor defined as such. The term "god" is a title of an entity that exists within a hierarchy of beings and has nothing to do with the Creator.

3. Race is the religion of the New World Order. People who sincerely believe in "race" and advocate categorization of the human family by means of such are evil and mentally-ill in the eyes of the Esoteric Black Dragon Society. The true definition of race is one's astrological sign, which all physical characteristic fall under. It is for this reason that practitioners of the Black Dragon Society's sciences have created a distinct ethnic identity for themselves and have dismissed all human categorization based on "racial features" as a form of mental illness.

4. The Esoteric Black Dragon Society does not support criminal activity of any kind. Anyone seeking membership into our culture while

engaging in criminal activities will be excommunicated and reported to the authorities. Crime is a disease that can only be cured through the use of Shinto technology.

5. Within all forms of life is an aspect of the source of all things, which we define in The Esoteric Black Dragon Society as love. It is through the cultivation of the Art of Ninzuwu that this state of enlightenment in love can be achieved (Amenominakanushi-no-mikoto).

6. The Art of Ninzuwu is composed of two aspects, Esoteric Shinto and Yi Jing Sorcery. In the days of remote antiquity, these two aspects were considered to be one science and an "art" of its own. The Esoteric Black Dragon Society's mission is to ensure the survival of the Art of Ninzuwu.

7. While we respect individuals from all religious paths, practitioners of the Art of Ninzuwu enjoy a non-religious status. The spiritual practices of Ninzuwu should not be confused with religion and its separatist ideologies.

Index

Other Works Written
by
Warlock Asylum

The Ivory Tablets of the Crow

The Yi Jing Apocrypha of Genghis Khan

The Armor of Amaterasu Ohkami

The Oracle of Enheduanna

The Atlantean Necronomicon

The Dark Knight of Nyarlathotep

Brooklyn Geisha

Musical Works
(Messiah'el Bey & Steven Berson)

Kiss of the Immortal (Album)

There in America (Album)

ABOUT THE AUTHOR

Messiah'el Bey (also known as Warlock Asylum) is a Shinto Priest in the Art of Ninzuwu lineage. He conducts Ninzuwu ceremonies, healing sessions, and various workshops on Ninzuwu-Shinto practices. Bey has written a wide variety of works on Ninzuwu culture, and other aspects of mysticism and esoteric practices found in ancient China, Japan, and Mesopotamia.

20666015R00093

Made in the USA
San Bernardino, CA
18 April 2015